'GET YOUR SKATES ON'

A HISTORY OF PLYMOUTH'S
ROLLER SKATING RINKS
1874–1989

BY

DIANA LAWER

with best wishes
Diana Lawer

Three Towns Publishing

i

Diana Lawer is a History graduate of the College of St Mark & St John, Plymouth. An adult education tutor and chartered librarian, she has worked in Plymouth City Library's Local Studies Department and has a special interest in local history and in the social history of leisure. She is currently Secretary of Plymouth Postcard Collectors Club, the largest in the UK.

© Diana Lawer 2007

ISBN 978-0-9557442-0-4

First published December 2007

Published by
Three Towns Publishing
35 Higher Compton Road
Hartley
Plymouth
PL3 5HZ

Printed and bound in Great Britain by
The Printing Press
21 Clare Place
Coxside
Plymouth
PL4 0JW

CONTENTS

PART TWO

APPENDICES

Illustrations: *Many of the illustrations are from the author's own collection of old postcards. They are a valuable and often overlooked source for local and social history studies. While most postcard images produced over 70 years ago are now out of copyright the publisher, photographer, artist and date of each one, if known, has been recorded to avoid contravening copyright laws. Permission to use more recent photographs has been obtained and sources acknowledged.*

FRONT COVER

Top Left: Skating Couple
This skating couple appear on a card most likely issued in the Netherlands. No publisher is shown but it is Series No. 1256 next to the logo 'R&K' within a sunrise

Top Right: Temptation
A Raphael Tuck card in the Photochrome Series Roller Skating (No. 4801). It was sent in September 1910.

Bottom Left: Tag and tickets for the Ebrington Street Rink

Bottom Right: Millbay Rinkeries Skating Cinderella of March 3rd 1910.

BACK COVER

Top Left: Waltzing Couple
A sample roller skating postcard issued by David Allen & Sons to rink managers. These could be ordered in bulk from 1,000 at 30 shillings.

Top Right: Elegant Lady Skater
A sample of a rinking design which could be ordered from John Waddington Ltd.: posters for 6d each; postcards @ 15s 6d per 1,000

Skates Off!
Postcard No. 623 in the Kute Kiddies Series by the Inter-Art Co., London. The card was posted in October 1911

GET YOUR SKATES ON

FOREWORD

Skating has long been a popular pastime and one of the few sports where large numbers of enthusiasts are able to take part at any one time. In England the skating craze can be divided into three definite phases: the roller skating 'rinkomania' from the 1870s; the renewed popularity of 'rinking' – also roller skating – which took off again in the early 1900s; and the intense interest from the 1970s in skating on rollers, real ice or synthetic surfaces which was fostered by the world championship successes of John Curry, Robin Cousins and Torvill and Dean.

This study of the provision of public roller skating rinks in The Three Towns, Plymouth, Devonport and Stonehouse, covers the period from the early 1870s when the first roller rinks were opened. It continues through to the 20th Century with the demise of Plymouth's skating rinks at the advent of World War Two. There is also an account of the short-lived return of roller skating in the 1960s and 1980s.

The appearance of so many local roller skating rinks is in itself an interesting microcosm of The Three Towns' social history. In examining the demand for and provision of these early skating amenities for the local urban populace against the national background various important aspects of social change in the South West are revealed.

These include the age and structure of the population; class participation in sport; transport facilities; scientific invention; building acquisition and use; entrepreneurs' increasing financial involvement in the leisure industry; innovation in entertainment, and, above all, an insight into the social pleasures enjoyed locally by the Victorians and Edwardians.

ACKNOWLEDGEMENTS

I would like to thank all those who have kindly helped me with my research, lent postcards and photographs or have given me permission to use them. I am extremely grateful to all the following: Graham Brooks, David Elliott, Frank Gent, Dr Todd Gray, Steve Johnson's 'Cyberheritage', Julie Lawrence, Brian Moseley, for his excellent website *www.plymouthdata. co.uk*, and to Chris Robinson for the images of the Blitz from his worthy revised version of Twyford's *'It Came To Our Door'*.

Thank you, too, to Plymouth City Library staff - Local Studies and Reference Departments; the West Devon Record Office; Birmingham City Library, Ordnance Survey GB; and the *Evening Herald*.

Last but not least, a big 'thank you' to Jason, Jennie and Lee of The Printing Press who kept this whole project 'rolling along'. What a team!

A Chronology of the Three Towns' Rinks

1874
30 Nov   Volunteer Drill Hall at Millbay opens

1875
22 Feb   Albert Hall (or *Royal* Albert Hall) opens
28 Apr   Volunteer Drill Hall Rink Closes
16 Apr   Albert Hall lease shortly to expire
16 Dec   Rink opened at the Mechanics Institute, Devonport, by Brighton Roller Skating Company
          First advertisement appears for Buckland Hall Roller Skating Club

1876
6 Jan   Buckland Hall Rink opens
14 Feb   Albert Hall Rink re-opens with new floor
17/18 Apr Skating Rink set up at Easter Fete, Plymouth Cricket Ground
7 Aug   Open Air Rink, Westwell Street, opens
31 Aug   Fall of wall at St Andrew's Hall building site
22 Sep   Albert Hall re-opens early due to Westwell Street accident
9 Oct   Pavilion New Skating Rink opens in premises of Ginnett's Hippodrome & Circus
26 Dec   St Andrew's Hall Rink & Bicycle School, Westwell Street, opens

1880
May   Phoenix Hall rink opens

ALL THE ABOVE RINKS HAD CEASED OPERATING BY THE 1890s

1889
          Plymouth Pier Pavilion added. Sometime in 1889/90 roller skating is introduced here, continuing until 1937

1909
17 Sep   Ebrington Street Rink opens, skating continuing until Good Friday, 1921
11 Nov   Millbay Rinkeries opened, skating offered with Sunday music concerts; later wrestling and boxing introduced, all continuing until the 1941 Blitz.

CHAPTER ONE

THE BIRTH OF ROLLER SKATING

I acquired my first pair of roller skates when I was about eight years old. In the 1940s skates were not very sophisticated, my very first pair looking very similar to the original patented designs which had appeared 80 years earlier. My love of skating continued into my teens with visits to London ice rinks.

A pair of slightly rusted old-style roller skates, c.1950s, a type in use long before roller blades became popular

Another hobby of mine is postcard collecting and in the early 1970s I began to acquire cards of roller skaters and rinks. Then 30 years ago I took possession of a scrapbook of Plymouth's 'Rinkeries' and started to research this fascinating mass participation sport and the roller skating crazes which caught on in The Three Towns.

Where & when did skating start? Ice skating probably began in Scandinavia many centuries ago on frozen ponds and lakes when weather conditions were right. The very first skates were made from animal bone and, much later, from iron. Ice skating was very popular with young and old, rich and poor. Samuel Pepys ice-danced with Nell Gwynn during the Great Frost of 1683 and Napoleon Bonaparte, as a trainee soldier, nearly drowned in 1791 while skating, falling in the ice-covered moat at Fort Auxerre, France. Queen Victoria also had her own skates as a girl. People loved skating. It was great fun and a healthy, bracing, social activity. It was a pity that one couldn't skate all the year round.

Ice Skating Clubs were formed in Britain as early as the 1700s and in 1842 the Skating Club of London was founded and later ice skating as a sport was introduced into North America by British servicemen. In 1858 the first properly maintained rink was set up in New York's Central Park. In the 1860s ice skating really took off, not only in America and Canada but across all the colder countries of Northern Europe, but still only on outdoor, naturally frozen spaces.

Skating was so popular that experiments were carried out with artificial ice, a curious compound of soap and alum, boiled down and poured over the floor to simulate real ice. Rinks were set up at the Baker Street Bazaar and at the Coliseum in London but were a failure.[1] A few mechanically refrigerated rinks were devised, though these were very small. The very first in 1876 was the Glaciarium near the King's Road, Chelsea, measuring only 40 feet by 24 feet. Others were set up in a few large towns and cities but their upkeep proved too labour intensive and expensive.[2]

Better all weather facilities were needed to make skating a year round activity, especially larger indoor rinks with man-made surfaces that could be more easily maintained.

In the 1860s a new and novel form of skating emerged with the invention of a four-wheeled roller skate. This revolutionary skate design triggered the start of the craze known as 'rinkomania' which the Oxford English Dictionary defined as 'a passion for rink skating'.[3] However, by the late nineteenth century several other socio-economic factors came together throughout England to foster participation sports such as roller skating.

In The Three Towns[4] there was increasing urbanisation and a rapidly growing and relatively youthful population. Regulation of employment hours gave a shorter working week which together with a marked rise in real incomes allowed the lower and middle classes more free time and provided the cash for chosen leisure pursuits. The Victorians stressed the benefits of health-giving exercise and skating was ideal for this.

Improvements in transport and communications, the proliferation of provincial newspapers and their widespread advertising and reporting of local events, and technological advances, all fostered the development of organised recreation. By the end of the nineteenth century better wages, more free time, improved transport systems, local newspaper advertising and new technology all combined to promote a flourishing, profitable leisure industry, setting up all the right conditions to bring about a new sporting craze.

It is therefore not surprising that roller skating, the only mass participation sport that Victorians and later the Edwardians could enjoy, became very popular in the lively and rapidly expanding area that was The Three Towns,

Although the Victorian craze of rinkomania declined by the turn of the century enthusiasm for roller skating was revived in 1909 with the popularity of 'rinking'. Almost every large town had its roller skating venue and The Three Towns' inhabitants were again to enjoy this energetic exercise at three well known and go ahead establishments, two of which continued well into the 1930s.

Roller skating in The Three Towns and in Plymouth, although quite well documented, has not previously been recorded. Written reports and pictorial evidence, however, do give a unique insight into the fun and pleasures of this exhilarating sport.

A view of the densely populated district of Ford with Devonport Dockyard in the background. The card was published by Valentines in the early 1900s.

The Royal Naval Engineering College, Keyham, published by Stengel & Co of Dresden and Berlin. It was posted from Devonport on 6 December 1905

CHAPTER TWO

SETTING THE SCENE FOR RINKOMANIA

POPULATION

The first roller rink in the UK opened at Brighton in 1874. Most large towns followed suit and, as was to be expected, The Three Towns was no exception. There were many reasons why roller skating became really popular here, not least that the area had a lively and growing population.

Plymouth, Devonport and Stonehouse, with the adjoining districts of Stoke, Morice Town and Ford, were known collectively as 'The Three Towns'. Situated on the eastern boundary of the Cornish peninsular this 'Metropolis of the West' was the largest conurbation in the south west, as the city of Plymouth still is today.

The growth and prosperity of the region was linked directly to its maritime position. There was a thriving fishing industry, but primarily The Three Towns was a naval and garrison town with a large Naval dockyard. In the nineteenth century the regular influx of visiting sailors boosted the already large numbers of service personnel stationed there including Royal Marines, students of the Royal Naval Engineering College at Keyham (1880-1959)[1], and boy ratings based on the various training ships in the Sound.

The Three Towns was the Headquarters of the Military Commander-in-Chief, Western District, which covered more than a dozen counties.[2] It was the base for several visiting regiments and was also the home of the Royal Engineers, the Royal Artillery, and the 3rd Battalion the Devonshire Regiment. Local barracks invariably housed upwards of 2,000 troops. The 1901 census shows that over 12,000 army and navy personnel were stationed there at that time. Skating rinks were to prove very popular with this group as members of the armed services were to make up a substantial proportion of the skating rinks' clientele.

Furthermore, late nineteenth century Plymouth was becoming increasingly popular as a holiday resort amongst the middle and upper classes. Visitors arrived by steamship and train staying in large hotels, many being in close proximity to the urban skating rinks. These included the imposing neo-gothic Duke of Cornwall built by railway directors in 1865 to cater for the influx of visitors keen to enjoy the local bracing air, picturesque scenery and leisure amenities.

The Duke of Cornwall Hotel in the early 1900s. The pre-1918 card was printed locally by Bowering & Co. and was not postally used.

H. M. Training Ship „Impregnable"   Plymouth Harbour

HM Training Ship Impregnable, Plymouth Harbour. She was an old 121-gun ship of 1860 formerly named HMS Howe. The ship, which still had the figurehead of Lord Howe, was renamed HMS Bulwark before she became the Impregnable in 1886. In 1891 she was commissioned at Devonport as the training ship HMS Caledonia and thereafter based at Queensferry on the Firth of Forth. This unused postcard is by Stengel & Co.
(Dave Elliott collection)

The population of The Three Towns rose dramatically in seven decades from just under 44,000 in 1801 to over 132,000 by 1871 with corresponding rapid urbanisation of the area. In the 60 years from 1851 the population doubled and by 1911 had reached over 200,000, boosted by visiting service personnel and the growing number of tourists.

The table (below), compiled from census figures, shows just how quickly the population grew. These figures do not include numerous residents in nearby districts just beyond the urban boundary or those in more outlying places such as Ivybridge or further afield in East Cornwall nor did they take into account the many holiday visitors.

POPULATION OF THE THREE TOWNS (Every 20 years from 1851)

YEAR	PLYMOUTH	DEVONPORT	STONEHOUSE	TOTAL
1801	16738	23747	3407	43892
1851	52933	38180	11979	103092
1871	68758	49449	14585	132792
1891	88931	55946	15401	161278
1911	112030	81678	13748	207456

There was a varied class structure in The Three Towns and all sections of society were to enjoy skating as a pastime. The 'upper class' consisted of a small stratum of landed aristocracy and an older 'officer elite' who used their wealth to 'buy' commissions. The middle class held a new breed of 'career officer' who came up through public schools and a core of affluent business and professional men, lawyers, bank managers, civil servants and their families. The lower middle classes made up a sizeable and growing section of, for example, shopkeepers, teachers, dockyard managers and clerks, as would be expected in any large town.

A substantial proportion of the population was working class, the largest number of workers employed in the Royal Naval Dockyards. There were upwards of 3,000 men at Devonport by 1873 and nearly 8,000 in the Dockyard and Keyham Steam Yard by 1902. Other workers were occupied in the thriving fishing industry, in building trades, and in domestic service.

Evidence of a much higher ratio of working class compared to other towns like Exmouth and Torquay can be seen from a study of the 1901 Census which reveals a much lower percentage of wealthy households with servants in The Three Towns.

PROPORTION PER CENT OF FEMALE DOMESTIC SERVANTS
TO SEPARATE OCCUPIERS OR FAMILIES at 1901 Census:

E. Stonehouse	Plymouth	Devonport	Exmouth	Torquay
12.2	17.6	10.9	43.2	42.8

Admittedly skating appeared to be more of a middle class pastime as can be seen by the number of evening dress functions held, but many of the workers in The Three Towns could be considered as a 'labour aristocracy', holding similar values and emulating the life styles of their middle class counterparts. They would therefore not feel out of place sharing the same amusements. Furthermore, John Brock, manager of the Millbay Rinkeries (from 1909) often sent out invitations to commanding officers of regiments inviting them to send along their men to join in the skating fun.

The character and population of an area is bound to have some bearing on the type of leisure pursuits offered and ensures the success of mass recreation. An analysis of the age structure of Plymouth and Devonport reveals a predominately youthful cross section who would welcome an energetic pastime. In Plymouth and Devonport in 1901 more than 80 per cent of the population were aged between 10 and 45 years. All these young people needed some form of healthy exercise and entrepreneurs who provided leisure facilities were not unaware of this huge potential consumer market.

NEW BASIN, KEYHAM DOCKYARD, DEVONPORT.
OPENED BY T.R.H. PRINCE AND PRINCESS OF WALES, FEBRUARY 21ST, 1907.

A card published by WG Swiss & Sons, Marlboro Street, Devonport, to commemorate the opening of the New Keyham Basin on 21 February 1907

WAGES AND HOURS OF WORK

What standard of living did the working classes enjoy? How well paid, for example, were naval and dockyard personnel? Did they receive sufficient wages to have money to spare for recreation? Taking the year 1875 as an example, *The Navy List* for that year *(See Appendix I)* shows that sailors' pay scales ranged from a meagre 7d. per day for a Band Boy up to three shillings a day for a Chief Carpenter's Mate, though each member of a ship's company would receive free board and lodging. An Able Seaman – a trained sailor – received 1s.7d. per day, all found, though he did have to provide his own soap and tobacco, and this rose to 1s.9d. for a Leading Seaman. Sailors' weekly rates of 11s.1d. and 12s.3d. respectively seem rather low, but they were probably adequate enough to finance a pint or two and a few sessions at the rink!

Dockyard workers were much better paid. The 'elite' of the workforce – salaried officers who were paid quarterly – could earn as much as £300 to £500 a year, and merited housing allowances of between £35 and £75 per annum in lieu of allocated accommodation. The wages of skilled and unskilled workers in 1875 varied enormously. 'Look-out men', for example, earned as little as 2s.6d. per day on a seven-day scale, whereas others were on a six-day payment: draughtsmen earned 10s. per day; boilermakers from 6s. to 9s., and shipwrights from 6s to 11s., all dependent on ability, good conduct and length of service.[3]

Research into their pay scales reveals that annual income did compare favourably with national levels set out in the *Cost of Living Tables* compiled by George Barnsby and also with the average male wage as given in *Wood's Index. (See Appendix II)*

Allowing that most workers did have cash to spend on leisure activities, how much free time did they have for recreation after fulfilling their obligations at work? The *Western Daily Mercury* of 3 January 1870 set out the revised timetable for the Keyham Steam Factory. Arrival and leaving times were rigidly controlled by the ringing of a bell. A longer summer and a shorter winter timetable was operated to make use of natural daylight rather than expensive gas lighting. The rates of pay varied accordingly, much to the workers' annoyance. The total number of hours worked each week varied from 37 in winter to 52 in summer. However, when electric light was introduced at the turn of the century a uniform working week was possible.

In 1870 Dockyard employees were still having to work for two hours on a Saturday afternoon though they did have the morning free. By the

A Stengel postcard view (No.E25165) of Millbay Station, a stone's throw from many early roller rinks. The card was posted from Plymouth to Perrenwell Station on 17 August 1907.

A pre-1918 scene at Mutley Station, Plymouth, published by Hardings of Bristol & Cardiff in their Regal Series *No. 807*

Work is well under way on the erection of the Royal Albert Bridge in 1857. This important rail bridge link connecting Devon to Cornwall was opened in May 1859.

An early 1900s postcard showing Saltash Railway Station and the Royal Albert Bridge. It was published by J Welch of Portsmouth (No.1793)

mid-1870s this arrangement was changed so that they only worked the Saturday morning until 1.20pm.[4] On no day did they work later than 6pm. So workers would have had evenings, Saturday afternoons and all day Sunday free for leisure, these hours of recreation compatible with skating rink opening times. *(See Appendix III)*

Rinks also catered for families, young ladies and holiday visitors by holding afternoon sessions, though the Albert Hall reserved afternoons for subscribers and friends, as seen in the advertisement to announce that rink's opening.

TRANSPORT

Improved public transport in England was a boon to organised recreation as it brought many patrons to urban leisure establishments. By the time the first of The Three Towns' skating rinks opened a local transport system was well established.

An excellent rail network had developed which from the late 1840s began to penetrate the very heart of The Three Towns and its docks. *(Appendix IV)*. The South Devon Railway reached Laira, on the eastern outskirts of the region, on 5th May 1848 and was then extended to Millbay, this section opening on 2nd April 1849. (Millbay Rinkeries advertised as being 'one minute from Millbay Station'.) That same year Mutley station opened. Ten years later in 1859 Isambard Kingdom Brunel's Royal Albert Bridge carried a new line across the River Tamar into Cornwall and the branch line to Tavistock opened.

By 1876 the London and South West Railway linked Marsh Mills and Lydford to Plymouth and these services were soon extended to various outlying districts such as Turnchapel and Yealmpton. Around the turn of the century both the L.S.W.R. and the Great Western Railway inaugurated a pattern of suburban services, the latter opening many new halts and introducing steam rail cars in 1904.[5]

As well as trains The Three Towns had numerous trams. There had been private horse drawn buses in the 1830s, before the advent of roller skating rinks, but the first public tram service, operated by the Plymouth, Stonehouse & Devonport Tramways Company, commenced in 1872, the forerunner of many in operation by the early 1900s.

There were also two important passenger ferries and two smaller ferries linking Plymouth with East Cornwall. There had been a ferry at Saltash from early medieval times but the first steel ferry was introduced in 1891. This

A delightful photograph of two children in Ebrington Street while behind them a No. 7 horse bus, advertising Spooner's store and Fry's Cocoa, carries roof top passengers. *(Steve Johnson's Cyberheritage collection)*

A policeman keeps his eye on a group of youngsters, possibly schoolchildren, while a tram makes its way down Edgcumbe Street, Stonehouse. This card (No.E18691) was published by Stengel & Co of 39 Redcross Street, London. *(Dave Elliott collection)*

13

The Saltash Ferry coming over from the Plymouth side, carrying equipment for the 'Hippodrome Big Show'. There is no publisher or date shown but the card was probably produced before the 1920s.

became the reserve ferry when a larger vessel, also built by Willoughby, was introduced in 1911. The Torpoint Ferry operated as a formal service from 1791, changing to a chain ferry or 'floating bridge' in 1834. From 1917 both these ferries were free to servicemen wearing uniform.

The Millbrook Steamboat Company, owned by John Parson, bought the steamer *'Millbrook'* in 1885, operating services between Millbrook across the Hamoaze to North Corner, Devonport. In 1891 this landing point was transferred to the Mutton Cove Pier. The smaller Cremyll Ferry began as early as 1204 and was managed by the Edgcumbe family until 1943 when the Millbrook Steamboat & Trading Company took over. This ferry brought people from Cremyll in the parish of Maker (once known as West Stonehouse) to East Stonehouse which was in close proximity to the many roller skating rinks.

Better transport facilities in The Three Towns made life much easier for everyone and not least for the working classes. In Plymouth, even into the 1870s, some 'yardees' had been required to live not more than two miles from their dockyard place of work [6] but improved transport links soon made this ruling obsolete.

The population came to appreciate the advantages of a good public transport system across the whole area: the many local rail networks

A busy scene at the Torpoint Ferry on this unused 'Milton Series' postcard published by Woolston Bros. London, EC1

*A crowd of trippers waiting at the Cremyll Ferry on the Cornwall side is depicted on this unused pre-1918 card. The publisher is not named, the only clue being the trademark – a letter **W** within a diamond shape.*

including links across the Tamar, a reliable tram service, at first horse-drawn but later electrified, and motorised omnibuses. People utilised it all to the full for both work and leisure.

Leisure centre proprietors also took advantage of the excellent transport facilities, many running special trains or offering cheap tickets to convey devotees of music hall, circus, pantomime and sport into Plymouth from as far afield as Exeter, Exmouth, Teignmouth, Falmouth, Penzance and all intermediate stations.[7]

Great Western Railway.

Time Table of

MOTOR OMNIBUS SERVICE

BETWEEN

PLYMOUTH (Millbay Station), CROWNHILL ROBOROUGH and ROBOROUGH ROCK

From Monday, September 12th, 1904,

AND UNTIL FURTHER NOTICE,

A Motor Omnibus, with accommodation for Luggage,

Will run (condition of roads permitting) Daily, as under:

Names of Stations.				Week Days.						Sundays.	
		a.m.	a.m.	p.m.	p.m.	p.m.	p.m.			p.m.	p.m.
PLYMOUTH (Millbay Station)	dep.	9 0	11 0	2 0	5 0	7 15	10 0	......		2 30	6 30
COMPTON LANE END	,,	9 15	11 15	2 15	5 15	7 30	10 15	......		2 45	6 45
CROWNHILL BARRACKS	,,	9 22	11 22	2 22	5 22	7 37	10 22	......		2 52	6 52
GEORGE HOTEL	,,	9 30	11 30	2 30	5 30	—		......		3 0	7 0
ROBOROUGH VILLAGE	,,		11 38	2 38	5 38	—		......		3 8	7 8
ROBOROUGH ROCK	,,	—	—	A	A	—				3 25	7 25
ROBOROUGH ROCK	dep.	—	A	A	A	—		......		3 35	7 35
ROBOROUGH VILLAGE	,,	—	11 45	3 30	6 30	—				3 52	7 52
GEORGE HOTEL	,,	—	—	3 37	6 37	—		......		3 59	7 59
CROWNHILL BARRACKS	,,	9 38	12 0	3 45	6 45	8 8	10 30	......		4 7	8 7
COMPTON LANE END	,,	9 45	12 7	3 52	6 52	8 15	10 37	......		4 15	8 15
PLYMOUTH (MILLBAY STATION)	arr.	10 0	12 22	4 7	7 7	8 30	10 52	......		4 30	8 30

A Wednesdays and Saturdays only between Roborough and Roborough Rock.

THE SINGLE FARES WILL BE AS UNDER:

From	To Millbay Station.	To Compton Lane End.	To Crownhill Barracks.	To George Hotel.	To Roborough Village.	To Roborough Rock
MILLBAY STATION	—	2d.	2d.	6d.	8d.	1s
COMPTON LANE END	2d.	—	2d.	4d.	6d.	10d.
CROWNHILL BARRACKS	4d.	2d.	—	2d.	4d.	8d.
GEORGE HOTEL	6d.	4d.	2d.	—	2d.	6d.
ROBOROUGH VILLAGE	8d.	6d.	4d.	2d.	—	4d.
ROBOROUGH ROCK	1s	10d.	8d.	6d.	4d	

LOCAL NEWSPAPERS

Another nation-wide development which promoted mass recreation was the proliferation of provincial newspapers which sprang up from the early 1860s after the abolition of press and advertising taxes. Three important dailies serving The Three Towns – the *Western Daily Mercury* (1860-), the *Western Morning News* (1860-) and the *Western Evening Herald* (1895-) as well as the privately published *Western Figaro* (1877-) all carried extensive advertising for various amusements as well as reports of the actual events. This did much to publicise and popularise roller skating as a pastime. Many other newspapers in Devon and Cornwall also advertised amusements in The Three Towns and all regularly published timetables of local transport.

A splendid open-top vehicle carries representatives of the Western Morning News, the 'leading West of England daily'. Special promotional visits were made by the firm all round the South West. Here WH Bryant, Newsagent, of 76 High Street, Ilfracombe, has put on an impressive display for this occasion in 1910. The card was published by Major, Darker & Loraine, Photographers, Barnstaple, who had branches in other Devon locations, including Plymouth.

CHAPTER THREE

SKATE AND RINK DEVELOPMENT

TECHNOLOGICAL DEVELOPMENT

Nationally the one factor which governed the emergence of skating as a participation sport more than any other was technological development. Skating had for centuries been a popular healthy exercise combining skill and technique with the thrill of speed and action. However, enjoying the exhilarating sport of ice skating had only been possible when temperatures dropped low enough to ensure the necessary frozen surfaces.

There had been several attempts at designing a roller skate which could be used on flat surfaces other than ice. A Belgian, Joseph Merlin, is credited with the first invention of a type of roller skate in 1760. He chose to exhibit his new invention at the celebrated Mrs Cornelly's masquerade fancy dress soirée in Carlisle House, Soho Square, London, skating into the ballroom playing a violin. Unfortunately, because he could not change direction or check his speed, he crashed into a large £500 mirror and was badly injured which seemed to put an end to roller skate inventions for a while![1]

Robert Tyers' 'Rolito' skate, 1823

In 1819 a Frenchman, Monsieur Petibled, invented an inline skate to be used on the Parisian boulevards. However, surfaces proved too stony and his skates did not allow for the execution of turns and curves. Interest in his design soon waned but a few years later, on the 22nd April 1823, a fruiterer of Picadilly, Robert John Tyers, took out a patent on his 'Rolito' skates, demonstrating them on a tennis court at Windmill Hill. They had five small wheels arranged in a single line and were described as *'an apparatus to be attached to boots ... for the purposes of travelling or pleasure'.*[2]

In 1859 a Mr Woodward designed India rubber skate wheels. However, in a short time these became pressed out of shape by the metal surround. None of these skates could execute curves. It was not until the 1860s that improvements in skate design and artificial rink surfaces led to the

James L Plimpton, the pioneer of modern roller skate design

emergence of a national indoor craze for roller skating, popularly called 'Rinkomania'.[3]

The first practical four-wheeled roller skate was invented in 1863 by an American, James Leonard Plimpton (or *Plympton*, as it is sometimes spelt), the prototype for all subsequent modern designs.

His 'rocking action' skate or 'quad' skate had four wheels, a pair at the front under the ball of the foot and another pair at the rear under the heel. Using a system of rubber cushion pads between the wooden plate and the axles they allowed skaters to make curves, execute intricate figures, and to change direction by shifting one's weight from side to side without lifting the skates from the surface. His original skate had toe and heel clamps but a later 1866 model had straps and buckles.

Plimpton's skates could be used in all weathers, all year round, on tarmac and other hard surfaces outdoors or indoors. Plimpton, a furniture maker, installed a wooden skating floor at his furniture premises in New York City. He leased out his skates and in 1866 converted the ballroom of the Atlantic House in Newport, Rhode Island, into a public skating rink. He also founded the New York Roller Skating Association (NYRSA) to promote skating as a pastime and travelled across North East America giving skating lessons to novices and awarding medals to those passing a skating proficiency test. By 1870 his proficiency medals were being awarded in over 20 countries to skaters using Plimpton's skates.

This revolutionary invention triggered off 'rinkomania' in the USA[4] and led to the emergence of numerous large rinks across America which could accommodate as many as 1,000 skaters and 3,000 spectators at a time.

On 25th August 1865 a provisional specification for the Plimpton skate was left at the UK office of the Commissioners of Patents by an agent, Alfred Vincent Newton. Letters Patent No. 2190 were sealed on the 9th January 1866. *(See Appendix V.)* Working drawings *(See Appendix VI)* show the sophistication of these skates especially when comparisons are made with modern twentieth century designs.[5]

Although Plimpton's British patent was submitted in 1866 the American Civil War delayed the introduction of these skates from across the Atlantic into the UK. However, by the early 1870s the craze eventually reached Britain and the skates were being used in numerous rinks throughout England.

Local newspaper advertisements for rinks in The Three Towns constantly stressed the superiority of Plimpton's design. An advertisement for the Royal Albert Hall announced that *'Mr Martin has entered into arrangements to use the Plimpton skates by which the general public can pleasurably obtain a good substitute for ice skating'* and that *'a charge of 6d would be made for the use of each pair.'* [6] Another advertisement for this rink promoted *'Plimpton's celebrated skates, the same as used by the champion skaters at the rink and St James Hall for their wonderful evolutions.*[7]

Plimpton's superior invention and the skating craze it inaugurated led to a spate of English and foreign imitations and other so-called improvements. His American lawyers drafted a standard letter which was sent to anyone infringing his patent. The index of UK patentees for the 1870s reveals an incredible number of applications lodged by aspiring roller skate inventors. *(See Appendix VII.)*

A local advertisement in the *Western Daily Mercury* of 16 December 1875 announced the opening of yet another local rink and advocated the use of several of these new designs:

NEW SKATING RINK
The Brighton Roller Skate Company will open on
Thursday 16 December, 1875
At the Mechanics Institute, Devonport in the large Hall.
All the Brighton New Patent Skates will be introduced
Malcomson's Patent Steel
Keel Roller Skate
Bowle's Patent Spring Bar Flying Roller
'Victoria and Albert' Patent Roller Revolving Skate
Goddard's Patent Skate 'BELGRAVIA'
Spiller's Patent Regulator Skate[8]

Some of these 'pirate' roller skate inventors with their patent numbers and dates are listed below:

MALCOLMSON, H	Patent No.1620	no date	1874
SPILLER, A.F.	Patent No.2574	no date	1874
GODDARD, G.O.	Patent No. 783	3 March	1874
BOWLES, J.A.	Patent No.1402	17 April	1875
BOWLES, J.A.	Patent No.1403	17 April	1875
BOWLES, J.A.	Patent No.2852	13 August	1875 [9]

By the following year rink proprietors were using local newspapers to warn against inferior 'pirated' designs:

> **THE ALBERT HALL RINK, PLYMOUTH:** *Plimpton's roller skates only used. CAUTION: These skates are used in several rinks in the United Kingdom alone and they are the only satisfactory roller skates that can be used with perfect safety from risk of legal proceedings for infringement of patent …*

Patrons were notified in the press of successful and ongoing actions against Plimpton's imitators. The above 'caution' continues:

> *Instances can be given of persons who have suffered considerable loss by having first purchased other skates and afterwards have had to buy Plimpton's. The action against Malcolmson for infringing Plimpton's patent on the 27 January last decided on all points in Plimpton's favour, and no appeal was made. An action is still going on against Spiller & Co. and arrangements are being made for proceedings against other parties. For particulars apply to The Manager of the Devon & Cornwall Skating Rink Co. Ltd., 25 Courtney Street, Plymouth.[10]*

Inventors took up advertising space inserting endorsements to convince proprietors and users of the authenticity and legality of their own designs. Here one inventor, none other than Thomas Martin, proprietor of Plymouth's Albert Hall, does just that:

> *SKATES! SKATES! THE MARTIN PATENT SKATE. This unrivalled roller skate having been in use for eight months in many rinks in London and the provinces and having established its reputation as the only perfect skate that does not infringe the patent of Mr Plimpton and which has not been attacked by him, although he has been in possession of a pair of them for four months.*

The advertisement also states that a sample pair of skates would be sent on receipt of a P.O.D. for 35/-. Furthermore, Thomas Martin offered estimates for the fitting of rinks and gave his address as Northernhay Rink, Exeter.[11]

A local Plymouth man, brass founder William Wright, also designed a skate. His advertisement from the *Supplement to the Post Office Directory of Plymouth, Stonehouse & Devonport, 1867 is shown below.*

WILLIAM WRIGHT,
BRASS FOUNDER AND FINISHER,
Looe Street, Plymouth.

Old Fittings Re-Lacquered or Bronzed, equal to new.

All Orders executed with the utmost despatch.

He issued the following testimonial for his invention:

> To proprietors of skating rinks
> The Wright Roller Skate
> Protected by Patent
> Is the Simplest, the Fastest
> And the Strongest in Use.
> It cannot get out of order
> It bears without breaking
> The rough usage of learners
> For terms etc. apply to the inventor
> WILLIAM WRIGHT 3 Looe Street, Plymouth

A sample pair of skates would be sent to applicants on receipt of a 20/- postal order.[12]

William Wright's provisional specification No.3921 was dated the 11th November 1875 and Letters Patent No.4397 for an improved skate were sealed on the 16th June 1876. *(See Appendix VIII)* His original drawing shows the sophistication of this early skate. It is not known whether the skate proved popular and William Wright, Brassfounder, had moved from Looe Street to 37 Buckwell Street, Plymouth, by 1878.

Skate design was improved again by an American, Levant M. Richardson, in 1884 with the introduction of steel ball bearings into skate wheels. His design reduced friction, made skates lighter and easier to use and enabled roller skaters to perform even more intricate manoevres. In 1898 Richardson started the Richardson Ball Bearing and Skate Company

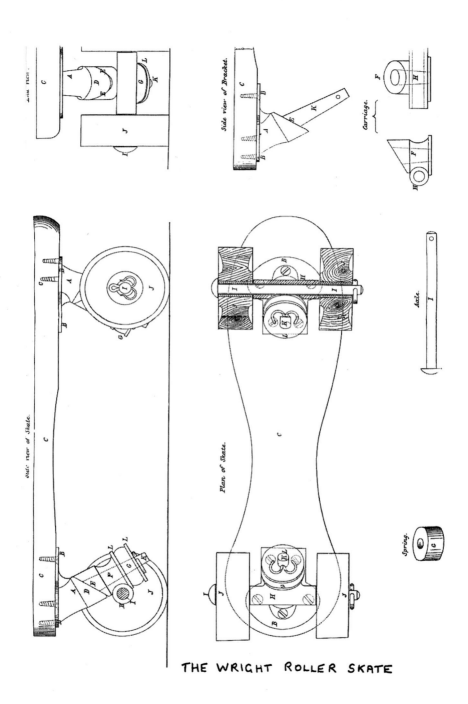

THE WRIGHT ROLLER SKATE

Roller Skates *all* sizes kept in stock

RULES FOR ROLLERS
"The beginner should be careful to get skates
that 'fit' his boots."

RULES FOR ROLLERS – The beginner should be careful to get skates that 'fit' his boots'
is the caption on this Valentine's Series card drawn by artist Lawson Wood. It was posted
from Truro to St Mellion on 1 January 1911.

which provided skates to most professional skaters of the time, including the speed skater Harley Davidson - no relation to the *Harley-Davidson* motorcycle company.[13] The Edwardian rink at Millbay used Richardson's skates exclusively which were *'adjusted weekly by an experienced skate mechanic kept expressly for that purpose.'*[14]

Early skate designs had toe clamps and strap fastenings and skates were manufactured in only a few sizes. Later the skate chassis was able to be adjusted in length, making it easier for rinkers with large or small feet to adjust their skates accordingly. Some skates were manufactured attached to leather boots, as most of them are today, but one had to know the correct size when hiring them at the rink. Toe-stops were introduced as early as 1876, but they were not commercially produced until the 1940s.

According to a press report young ladies at a local rink seemed to have had a problem with their footwear:

> *A person accustomed to roller skates can always tell you what size boot he takes – a feat quite beyond the reach of non skaters. Till roller skating was invented whoever heard of a person knowing the size of his boots? Certainly they did not. And they never will. On Saturday there was such a rush for number nines that several young*

RINKERS' RINKLES.

It will be found much easier and quicker to master the Art of Skating if Ball-bearing Skates are used from the start.

———

Bear in mind the fact that shoes should not be worn when Skating, as they form no kind of support for the ankles.

———

Boots of a heavy pattern will be found most suitable for Ladies, with heels similar to those of the English walking boot, and not on any account should the French heels, so popular amongst the fair sex, be worn.

———

Boots for Gentlemen should not be of too light a pattern, as the grip of the Skate is liable to pinch the foot if the sole of the boot is at all slender.

38

In fixing Skates it must be remembered that the axle of the front wheels should be immediately under the ball of the foot, and the back wheels well under the heel.

———

Don't look at the floor when Skating. Skate with the leg slightly bent at the knee, always keeping the weight more on the heel than the toe. Place each Skate down firmly, so that all four wheels touch the ground at the same time.

———

Don't skate too hurriedly. Fast skating is all very well for those who intend entering for speed contests ; but slow movements, with a good interval between each stride, are far more easy and graceful.

39

Instructions on acquiring and fitting the most suitable skates were given in this 1910 booklet 'Rinking: How-Where-When' together with some useful tips on skating technique.

ladies who came late had to make themselves happy on 9½s, which they declared to be 'immense things'.[15]

Other technological improvements which made skating more enjoyable in The Three Towns as elsewhere in England included supports to aid the beginner such as 'the 'Patent Safety Rinker' advertised by the Pavilion New Skating Rink as being *'supplied without charge that beginners may learn to skate easily with perfect safety, it being impossible to fall down'* [16]

RINK SURFACES AND DECOR

Skating surfaces were also improved. In the early years of organised roller skating in America and Europe rinks were set up outdoors on rough ground or on badly laid asphalt. Later, owners of large halls went to great lengths to ensure that skating surfaces were perfectly smooth and frequently shut down rinks temporarily to renovate and improve the floor and other amenities.

An early electric sanding and polishing machine used to bring wooden roller skating surfaces to tip-top condition.

The Pavilion New Skating Rink favoured asphalt but the proprietors of the Albert Hall Rink and the rink at Millbay's Volunteer Drill Hall preferred polished, hard pitched pine, the latter installing *'an entirely new floor ... of pitched pine, a perfect level being secured with considerable care. The floor too has a spring which is a great advantage.'* [17] Other rink owners across the UK favoured cement or maple.

The quality of a rink's surface was most important and caused much anguish if it fell below certain high standards. On a visit to the Millbay Rinkeries in November 1909, just after this rink opened, one of the rink's Directors, Mr HF Blackwell, had been *'disporting himself on the rink and had a few remarks to convey to the company's patrons and others.'*

> *'On behalf of the company,'* he said, *'I want to apologise to the public. We were not familiar with the current used with the surfacing machine, so that we were not able to get the floor properly treated for the opening week. We have had the machine working every night for the past week, and tonight we shall finish. I can conscientiously say that the floor is now in a better condition than that of any rink*

on which I have been for the last six months, and I have been on something like two hundred.' He concludes: *'I have no fear of the success of this rink.'*

The décor and atmosphere of the rinks was also very important and lighting played a major part in making the rinks attractive. The Albert Hall was lit with 'limelight effects' – light produced by a blow-pipe flame directed against a block of quicklime. Electric light, replacing the old gas lamps, was introduced after the turn of the century in many entertainment establishments.

This small orchestra was photographed at the Empire Rink, Bramall Lane, Sheffield. It was not usual practice to have musicians on the skating floor!

Live orchestras or brass bands were still employed at the Edwardian rinks for dances and 'cinderellas' but a modern gadget, the *Stentorphone,* was introduced at Millbay Rinkeries on Monday 5th May 1913 to provide musical accompaniment to the skaters' movements and for the enjoyment of spectators.[18] The attributes of the *Stentorphone* are described in a Press report headed *'A REMARKABLE INSTRUMENT'.*

By special invitation of the management of the Millbay Rinkeries, many interested musical friends, and several members of the local Press, were present at a private performance given yesterday by one of the most remarkable gramophones ever heard in the West of England. This magnificent instrument is of gigantic proportions, and

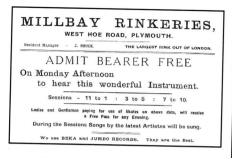
without doubt, one of the largest in the Provinces. Mr J Brock, the popular manager, ever ready to give his patrons something new, recently journeyed to London and, after hearing it, at once decided to have one installed at the rink.

The most noticeable feature is its wonderful clearness of tone, with an absence of the usual scratchy sounds. A special platform has been built at the lower end of the large rink, and over the instrument is a very large sounding board, which distributes the music well throughout the building. The recital was in every way satisfactory. Upwards of 300 of the very latest selections can be obtained, including Rag-time waltzes, songs, bands, marches, etc., and Mr Brock has already acquired upwards of 90 as a start.

It will be an acquisition to the rink, and rinkers will enjoy it to the full, distant music when light skating during the summer months is indulged in. The instrument is electrically driven, and with the exception of a little time regulation, is perfect. It will be used at each session daily, starting on Monday next when patrons will thoroughly enjoy this latest musical innovation.[19]

Rink proprietors in the Victorian and Edwardian eras had to keep abreast of all the latest developments to maintain the popularity of their establishments. But they also had to ensure that their rinks were profitable.

RINK BUSINESS AND PROFITS

This new form of amusement gave financiers and rink entrepreneurs the opportunity to reap considerable profits. The Victorian rinking commentator, JA Harwood, criticised the large sums being made from this latest development in the leisure industry at the expense of the skating public:

> *Companies and individuals who are fortunate to own rinks are really making too enormous profits – the ratio is 300 per cent – far larger than is considered sufficient or even advisable, for tradesmen to make.* He continues: *There is no reason to doubt that a system based on a smaller scale of gain would be more politic as tending to prolong the popular desire for this kind of entertainment.'*

He believed that proprietors would continue to charge too much and even though skaters would be silly enough to pay inflated prices, this would eventually cause *'some abatement in the present fervour in a short time.'* [20]

He adds that if charges were reduced skaters could practice the art more frequently, become more proficient and reap more health benefits.

However, most rink proprietors in The Three Towns did try to keep prices down, the Albert Hall offering packets of admission tickets at reduced prices and the Pavilion New Skating Rink advertising discounted family tickets at 10 for three shillings and sixpence.

Local skating clubs were also formed, the subscribing members being allowed to skate at certain allocated times and at reduced cost.

Chapter Four

The Art of Roller Skating and Its Benefits

Skating Technique

The art of roller skating was a new technique to be mastered and Plymouth's local press lost no time in giving out advice to budding skaters. This article in the *Western Daily Mercury* of 1st December 1874, written in elaborate Victorian prose, contained some handy hints and warnings for novices:

> *Plimpton's American patent skates are the only roller skates invented which allows the wearer to make curves. With them the wearer can cut figure eights as easily on the pitch pine floor as one with ordinary skates can do so on ice.*

> *Roller skating can no more be learnt in a day than can skating on ice; and it is only those who think they can, and go at it impetuously, that get the falls. A tyro [a novice], who rushes into roller skating heedlessly, is great fun. Mackney's clog dancing is nothing to it. The impetuous skater makes the whole rink his platform, is at one end before he knows he has visited the other, and finally accomplishes a breakdown surprising to himself and moving to the beholders.*

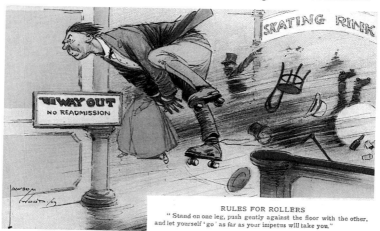

RULES FOR ROLLERS
" Stand on one leg, push gently against the floor with the other, and let yourself 'go' as far as your impetus will take you."

Another Lawson Wood card in the Valentine's Series RULES FOR ROLLERS. 'Stand on one leg, push gently against the floor with the other, and let yourself 'go' as far as your impetus will take you.' *The card was not postally used.*

The cautious skater closely watches the 'Professor', learns to walk before he attempts to run, and, gaining confidence, soon traverses the rink without saluting 'Mother Earth'. Of course there will be falls in roller skating, but they need only to be serious to the incautious, and at the worst the pleasure and recreation of a perfect skater is worth all the hard knocks it may cost him to accomplish it.

At the rink there is a professional skater who is ever ready to give all needful instruction; and the grace and ease with which he moves about is in itself a great incentive to visitors. The Professor has the very poetry of motion. Now he shoots straight down the rink as an arrow from a hard strung bow; suddenly he makes a grand sweep at the bottom and is up again; now he reaches the bottom in a course describing the line of beauty, and returns in a zig-zag of curves; now he is away on one leg, and now on another; now he turns within his own length as they say of handy ships, and shoots away with his face to the spectator, and finally surprises all by going the whole length of the hall sitting on one heel, holding his other leg in his hands, and gracefully curves at the bottom. [The journalist's use of Naval jargon here would have been well received by The Three Towns' readers!] *The Professor is, therefore, a worthy teacher of a most invigorating, health-giving accomplishment, and some of his pupils have already made great progress.'*

This local postcard of a skating 'professor', issued by Jerome of Union Street, Plymouth, was found in John Brock's Millbay Rinkeries Cuttings Book. *It has the dates* '1893 or 4' *written in ink on the reverse but is most probably later than this.*

32

A comic postcard, one of many in a roller skating series published by Henry Garner of Leicester. The card was sent from Exeter to Newton Abbott on 18 October 1920 by Jim who has added 'here in the barracks' *to the caption* 'We're all learning to skate'.

Yet another postcard in a 'Rinking' *series, this one published by the Philco Publishing Co. is No. 4105. The card was not posted but the message to Helen from George reads:* 'Please don't take all the cushions when you go on the rink'.

The following year another report extolled the virtues of skating but also criticised those who took the art to extremes! The article in Plymouth's *Western Daily Mercury* entitled *'The Plymouth Skating Rink'* by 'Non Skater' appeared on 23 November 1875.

> *'A person who has never had a run on a good field of ice has missed one of the greatest pleasures this world can afford. When I speak of skating I mean going right ahead, covering the greatest distance in the shortest time. Of course, there are people who prefer scientific skating, and these form skating clubs and make a regular business of their pleasure.*
>
> *A glance at a work on 'figure skating' by Messrs. Vandervell and Witham of the London Skating Club is enough to frighten one. The book contains many dreadful diagrams covered with explanatory letters of the alphabet, painfully reminding boys of that hard old man, the late Mr Euclid. No doubt the man who can do the 'double grapevine' and the 'double roses' on skates has the same talent as the man who can do the double shuffle in clogs. But he will never persuade an impartial observer that his 'figures' bear the slightest resemblance either to grapevines or roses ...*

ETIQUETTE FOR SKATERS:
THE GENTLEMAN SHOULD ALWAYS COME A CROPPER FIRST, AND THEN ASSIST THE LADY TO COLLAPSE GRACEFULLY.

A beautifully drawn postcard by an unidentified artist entitled ETIQUETTE FOR SKATERS. *The caption reads:* 'The gentleman should always come a cropper first, and then assist the lady to collapse gracefully!' *It was published by Bamforth (Series No. 2054) and was not postally used.*

'Non Skater' adds:

> There is a peculiar fascination about skating. When you are tired
> out you feel that you must have just one turn more. And so you take
> it and come down heavily, which makes your face look like a penny
> mask that has been kicked about by a lot of boys.'

In 1879 the *National Skating Association* was formed and many rinks,
including those of The Three Towns, became affiliated members, a
development in skating which legitimised the pastime as a recognised
sport.[1] The NSA laid down a rigid code which was accepted nationwide.
(See Appendix IX) Once moulded, these rules scarcely changed and
were still strictly adhered to throughout the next 'rinking' craze of the early
1900s. The Millbay Rinkeries was the only provincial Edwardian rink at
which all the skating figures were marked out in accordance with the NSA.
The manager, John Brock, was *'at all times pleased to show the various
figures executed in the correct style'.*[2] All rinks displayed rules for skating
discipline on large placards suspended from the ceiling and stewards were
engaged to enforce them and ensure they were obeyed. Instructors, too,
had their own rules to comply with while they were in the employ of the
skating rinks. *(See Appendix X)*

*One of Bamforth's comic rinking cards in Series No. 1463, which shows a collage
of skating figures superimposed onto a rink background. Note the rules for skaters
suspended from the ceiling, a practice common to most rinks.
The card was posted on 11 March 1910.*

Numerous 'rinking' postcards appeared from 1908 with the renewed roller skating craze including comic and artist-drawn cards depicting hilarious situations and awkward accidents. At this time postcard collecting was a national hobby, and the years from 1900 to around 1918 have been named the 'Golden Age' of postcards. This period just happened to include Edwardian 'rinkomania'.

Two postcards headed ROLLER SKATING in the National Series, *a trade name used by publishers Millar and Lang of Glasgow,* 'Oh dear, it's so slippy' *(No. 1140) is postmarked 27 May 1913.* 'His First Attempt' *(No. 1141) is unused.*

A HEALTHY EXERCISE

Contemporary writers commenting on this new sport often alluded, sometimes in an odd way, to the health-giving benefits of skating as does J. A. Harwood who, in his classic 1876 treatise entitled *Rinks and Rollers* supporting this new activity, decreed:

> *Let the visit to the rink take the place of the purposeless carriage drive or the objectless walk. Notice the air of those who rink daily. Contrast their clear complexions with the pale flabbiness of those who only vary the unusually unhealthy conditions of modern existence with an occasional walk round never-ending terraces of shops or stucco. Can there be a better advert for the rinks?[3]*

Harwood advocates the overall health advantages of skating,

> *'not only to the young ladies, but to the hard worked professional men, daily exercise would prove of great benefit. Their time is to them money and they are unable to take long weeks off to counterbalance their mental toil.*

He states, furthermore, that: *The paterfamilias who sits at home and grumbles over his port 'You are all rink mad' would benefit by a little plain-sailing skating.'[4]*

However, Harwood also points out the dangers in increased doctors' bills as the result of skating in the closed atmosphere of rinks, of the many injuries and broken bones, and the folly of young girls, and even old ladies, who skate with their hands in muffs and hit the floor hard with no free hands to steady themselves![5]

Victorians were very health conscious and local reporters in The Three Towns' Press frequently extolled the virtues of this invigorating exercise. In the same *Western Morning News* article of 23rd November 1875 'Non Skater' leaves readers in no doubt of the benefits of roller skating.

Doctors admit that there is no more healthy exercise than skating. The tumbling down and the getting up again, which tumbling down necessitates, bring all the muscles of the body into action and promote a vigorous circulation of the blood. Bilious people should therefore skate, so should chilblainey people, so should people who dine.[6]

ROLLERSKATING IS A MOST INVIGORATING AND HEALTHY EXERCISE.

A comic rinking card in the Kismet Series *(no. 143) posted from London to Penzance on 30 June via Buryas Bridge, Cornwall, with a second postmark dated 1 July 1911. The postcard is by an unknown artist who uses the pseudonym 'Syd'.*

The popular music hall star, Phyllis Dare, goes a-rinking wearing her muff! This Rotary Photographic card No. 11599 was posted in Fulham on 12 December 1910

THE BELLE OF THE RINK

'The Belle of the Rink' *is dressed in all her finery – exquisite dress, large hat – for a skating Cinderella or Carnival. The card in Millar & Lang's* National Series *was posted in Bradford on 26 August 1909. The message reads:* 'Hope to see you at the Rink on Saturday. If I see anything like this I shall know which is you. Trusting not to be disappointed as I am all of a flutter, from you know who.'

A more subdued outfit for this young lady who wears a typical costume for daytime rinking.

There can be no doubt that for the local populace skating was considered 'an invigorating and health-giving exercise' and local commentators maintained that skating was an *'invaluable institution … to the class whose recreation is at present least provided for – we mean the class which is subjected to close confinement during working hours …'* [7]

This appears to be a direct reference to the large and growing sector of lower middle class 'white collar' workers of The Three Towns. The health aspect of the sport, constantly stressed in the press, was also advocated in rinking booklets such as one produced locally in 1910. [8]

However, the journalist 'Non Skater' had his own unusual views on women skaters!

> *Skating is not only a healthy but also a very graceful exercise. Indeed, in this respect it is perhaps superior to dancing. Most women look well on horseback but they generally look better on skates. If I were part proprietor of a dozen daughters I should like to see them going about my house on Plimpton patent rollers.* [9]

Roller skating was 'especially agreeable to the ladies' although quite often modesty and decorum were lost after falling on the floor! They invariably practiced the sport in heavy, full length dresses and enormous, elaborate hats which must have hampered their style. The other new energetic craze, cycling, was also undertaken by females in unsuitable but elegant day wear.

New fashions came around such as the harem skirt (c.1911) which were purported to be less restrictive for skating. However, in time special sports outfits were designed for women and shorter skirts allowed them to move about more freely and gracefully.

When Mary went upon the Rink
And came a fearful cropper,

The Boys, who rushed to see the fun,
Said, "Harem Skirts ain't proper."

The Harem Skirt was introduced to the fashion world by designer Paul Poiret in his 1911 Paris Spring Collection. This style was far less cumbersome to skate in but it did give rise to many comic postcards. This Valentine's Series card was sent from Bridgend to Cardiff

By the 1920s ladies' skating outfits were shorter and much more practical. An instructress is seen here with her male colleague and a lady rinker poses for her own postcard portrait at the Novelty Studio, 184 Union Street, Plymouth

A Social Revolution

Harwood maintained that Plimpton's skate design brought a new kind of freedom, that it was

> *'nothing less than a social revolution. People meet at the rink in a way in which they meet nowhere else – I do not mean in collision! They meet others, form acquaintances or cement friendships that may or not be desirable, for example unauthorised or forbidden friends and lovers.'*

He mentions critics of rinking whose

> *'general outcry against the morality of the thing is that this flirtation ground must be abolished'* and that *'parents were furious at having the chance of selecting their children's partners wrested from them.'*[10]

It is clear that roller skating was to bring changes both in attitudes to health and in social conduct. Rinks became a new milieu for young people of both sexes to meet, unfettered by the too close attentions of chaperones. Many quite saucy postcards on this theme appeared depicting flirty situations and embracing couples!

SKATING IS A VERY EM-BRACING PASTIME

'Skating is a very em-bracing pastime' *is the caption on this card published by Henry Garner. Sent from Northampton to Leicester on 7 April 1909 the message contains the warning* 'Hope you won't start skating!'

HINTS TO SKATERS.
Avoid flirting when her Papa's about!

SHE (LEARNING) "NOW PROMISE YOU'LL NEVER LEAVE ME"

HE "OH MISS SMITH! THIS IS SO SUDDEN"

REGISTERED COPYRIGHT
No. 9381/4

'Hints to Skaters. Avoid flirting when her Papa's about!' *says it all. There was certainly a new social freedom at the skating rinks. This unused real photographic card is by Davidson Brothers.*

Romantic liaisons at the rink was the theme on many comic postcards. This one published by William Ritchie and Sons in their Reliable Series *(No.9381/4) was not postally used*

"I WISH SHE'D DO THIS WITH HER SKATES OFF"

Another beautifully drawn Bamforth card (No.2053), artist unknown. It was posted from Parkstone, Dorset, to Bournemouth on 1 October 1910.

The craze also provided a place where family members, young and old, could all take part in healthy exercise together. Furthermore, it also served to bring together different classes and ranks, the fun of skating helping to break down the restrictive social barriers prevalent in both the Victorian and Edwardian age.

THE CHAMPIONS.
Little pair with style so neat,
They are champions hard to beat.

One example from a delightful series of cards showing child skaters. Published by EA Schwerdtfeger & Co. (No.2406) it was sent from Stalybridge to Ashton-under-Lyne on 2 September 1910.

A skating line-up of the Moses family at the Millbay Rinkeries in May 1933. The photo was taken by Jerome of Union Street

CHAPTER FIVE

'RINKOMANIA' HITS THE THREE TOWNS!

The Three Towns was certainly not slow in getting in on the roller skating act! Local people had already had a taste of the art, watching famous American skating stars in music hall turns at the St James Hall.[1] Proprietors utilised existing large buildings for the purpose and with the rapid urbanisation of The Three Towns there was no shortage of immense halls in which to accommodate the sport. Often they erected purpose-built rinks, going to great lengths to equip them for the comfort and enjoyment of both skater and spectator. By the end of the 19th century nine different roller skating venues had been set up.

THE VOLUNTEER DRILL HALL, MILLBAY

In 1874 The Three Towns' very first skating rink opened. The *Western Daily Mercury* acknowledged that *'although little has been heard in the West of roller skating it has been in full operation in many towns in the east and north of England for twelve months'* and informed its readers, in the flowery rhetoric so typical of the Victorian press, that they were soon to have their very first roller rink.

> *'It is intended to open a skating rink in the Volunteer Drill Hall, Plymouth in a short time. This will enable the lovers of that most pleasant exercise to defy 'Jack Frost' and to display in his absence all the movements that they could upon ice. This will be especially agreeable news to the ladies who will, without risk or exposure to the inclemency and changeability of the weather, be able to enjoy this health-giving pastime.'*[2]

This first rink duly opened in the Volunteer Drill Hall on 30 November 1874.

In the 1870s the old Millbay Barracks, built in 1794 to house prisoners of war, became the headquarters of the 2nd Devon Volunteer Corps and a new drill-hall costing £2,000 was provided. Situated at Millbay it was a massive wooden structure with its entrance in Walker Terrace, between Prospect Place and West Hoe Road. The hall was frequently let for public use. It measured 260 feet long by 80 feet wide[3], but *'the area enclosed for the ice-defying skaters'* was 100 feet by 40 feet, *'considerably larger than the majority of skating rinks in the United Kingdom.'*

The high wall surrounding the Millbay Drill Hall, all of which has since been demolished.
(Picture courtesy of Steve Johnson's Cyberheritage)

This postcard shows the interior of the Drill Hall on the occasion of the 1905 Torrey
Alexander Mission held there. The photograph was taken by a
local photographer identified only by his initials 'TS'.

The manager, Mr Arundell Smith, sectioned off part of the hall and installed a new floor for the skating. The *Western Daily Mercury*'s lengthy, graphic report appeared the day after the opening and is reproduced below:

'With great éclat the skating rink opened and about 350 ladies and gentlemen, including many of the elite of The Three Towns and neighbourhood, attended the afternoon assembly, and witnessed the successful attempt to enjoy all the exhilarating recreation of skating without being at all dependent on King Winter who is rarely vigorous in his visits to the West.

Unfortunately, an accident to a well-known and much respected resident somewhat marred the proceedings, and it is better to mention it at the outset, for it should in no way create a prejudice against the later addition to the winter amusements of the neighbourhood, and the sufferer himself would be the last to wish that the untoward incident should have such an effect.

Colonel Elliott, Adjutant of the 2nd Battalion D.R.V. had only just had the skates put on before he slipped down easily but his leg falling under his body his ankle got hurt at a place where he once received an injury from a gunshot. The gallant Colonel wished to have the accident considered 'a mere nothing' and was at once removed to his house; and all must hope that he will soon be found gliding as gracefully down the rink, as does the 'Professor.'

The rink is under excellent management; the rules are simple and the 'hints' hung about should be mastered by the tyro before attempting. Even for those who care not to skate it is a very pleasant place to pass an evening. Rinks have done well in various parts of London, at Brighton, Cheltenham, Scarborough, and there is every indication of its being a success in Plymouth.[4]

From Monday 25th January the times of opening were altered to three two-hour sessions held daily at 11am; 3pm; and 7pm. Admission was one shilling, children under 12 paid 6d and skates could be hired for a sixpenny fee. Packets of 10 tickets were available at a reduced rate from Messrs. Moon & Sons or from Mr Sawday, George Street.

Sadly the Volunteer Drill Hall was short lived as a rink and closed after five months. This press notice issued by the managers appeared in the *Western Daily Mercury* on 28 April 1875:

> We are requested to state that the rink at the Drill Hall is closed owing to the proprietor not having been able to make arrangements with the Volunteer authorities.

The Drill Hall, besides being the home of the local Territorial Army, was also used for celebrity concerts in which famous singers such as Dame Clara Butt appeared, and for exhibitions, notably those organised by major hospitals in the 1920s.[5]

THE ROYAL ALBERT HALL, STOKE ROAD, ELDAD, STONEHOUSE

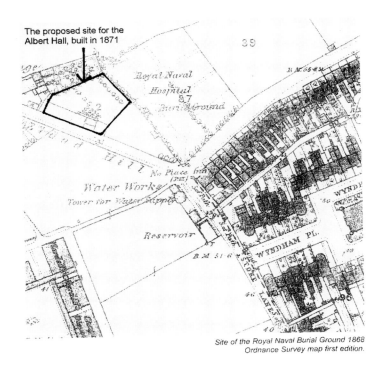

Site of the Royal Naval Burial Ground 1868
Ordnance Survey map first edition.

While managing the Drill Hall rink Arundell Smith opened his second rink in Plymouth on 22 February 1875, leasing the Albert Hall, sometimes referred to as the *Royal* Albert Hall, at Eldad, Stonehouse, from the proprietor, a Mr Thomas Martin.

The vast hall, which opened in September 1871, was on a large site adjacent to Stonehouse Mill. It backed onto the Naval Cemetery and was situated next to the No Place Inn.[6]

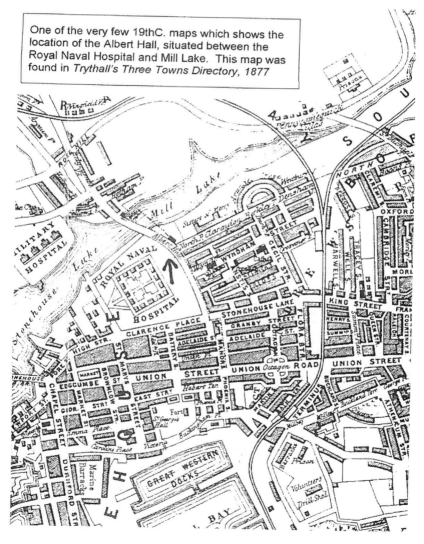

One of the very few 19thC. maps which shows the location of the Albert Hall, situated between the Royal Naval Hospital and Mill Lake. This map was found in *Trythall's Three Towns Directory, 1877*

A description of the building in the local press was not very flattering as it was said to have *'an exterior as unsightly as its interior is pretty and tasteful'*. Perhaps it is fortunate that no pictures exist now of this monstrosity! The builder, the very same Thomas Martin, was *'his own architect, contractor, builder, decorator and overlooker'*.[7]

It was originally intended to be used for concerts and could seat 2,800 with standing room for upwards of 4,000. It was 130 feet long by 80 feet wide; the central height was 40 feet and the floor area accommodated 1800 chairs. There were raised tiers on one side with a balcony at the other end and the whole was lit with an arch of gas jets.

This impressive hall was the most central concert venue of The Three Towns and was also the home of the famous Bonfanti's Circus. It staged music hall entertainment including Dioramas[8] of military events such as the Crimean War and the Indian Mutiny which were very popular with audiences. And imagine the delight of the local population when in 1871 the proprietor, a Mr Thomas Macallum, announced that he had

'succeeded in effecting an engagement, although at enormous expense, with the world renowned artist, the Great and Original Monsieur Blondin, the Hero of Niagara in his unapproachable and truly miraculous performance on the high rope 50 feet in the air.'[9]

Another playbill shows that as early as 1872, at a 'Grand Benefit Night' on Thursday 11 April, a troupe of American skaters, the Silbon Family, had appeared there in the 'Comic Entertainment' on the *'Summer'* skates', another patented design, a performance which no doubt created much local interest in this new form of recreation.

Mr Chevalier Blondin crossing Niagara in August 1859 with his manager Harry Colcord on his back.

This advertisement in the *Western Daily Mercury* announced the rink's opening:

The Monster Skating Rink
Will Open Monday February 22nd
The largest floor in the West of England
Three assemblies daily – Two hours each. Opening 11am., 3pm., 7pm.
The Morning and Evening Assemblies will be open to the. Public at 1s.
each including the use of Skates.
The Afternoon Assembly for Subscribers and Friends only
from whom a Committee of Management will be elected.
Subscription £1 1s for 30 Tickets, or £1 1s per month,
admissible to Morning, Afternoons, and Evening Assemblies
These charges include the use of skates
A BAND, under the direction of Mr. J. Fly
Will perform every Monday, Wednesday, and Saturday.
Tickets may be obtained of Messrs. Moon and Sons, or Mr Sawday,
George Street [10]

ROYAL ALBERT HALL PLYMOUTH.

THE MONSTER SKATING RINK

WILL

OPEN MONDAY, FEBRUARY 22ᴺᴰ

The largest floor in the West of England

THREE ASSEMBLIES DAILY for Two Hours each. Opening. 11 a.m., 3 p.m., and 7 p.m. The Morning and Evening Assemblies will be open to the public at 1s each, including the use of Skates. The Afternoon Assembly for Subscribers and Friends only, from whom a Committee of Management will be elected.

Subscription £1 1s. for 30 Tickets, or £1 1s. per month, admissible to Morning, Afternoons, and Evening Assemblies.

These charges include the use of skates.

A BAND, under the direction of Mr. J. Fly, will perform every Monday, Wednesday and Saturday.

Tickets may be obtained of Messrs Moon and Sons, or Mr. Sawday, Georgestreet.   6634

Although having lost the Drill Hall rink, the lessee Arundell Smith and proprietor Thomas Martin spared no effort or expense to make their 'Monster Skating Rink' at the Albert Hall a superior establishment. This report of the opening night of 22 February 1875 appeared the following day in the *Western Daily Mercury*:

There cannot be a doubt that roller skating is established among the amusements of Plymouth at least for the winter months. Three months since Mr Smith introduced it at the Drill Hall, and now the opening of a second rink has to be chronicled. For such a place the Albert Hall had many advantages, and in his present arrangements, Mr Martin has made much of them. He has done his best to make the amusement still more popular by providing a rink which in its arrangements and appearance contributes to the comfort and pleasure of skaters.

The side galleries have been removed and three-quarters around the hall runs a promenade overlooking the skating floor …The entrances have been improved and a retiring room for ladies has been added. The skating floor is nearly 90 feet long and between the pillars it is 40 feet wide. The floor is surrounded with tables and chairs – resting places for skaters and their friends. The hall has been decorated with great taste – scarlet and gold being the respective colours.

An entirely new floor has been laid of pitch pine, a perfect level being secured with considerable care. The floor too has a spring which is a great advantage. About 80 ladies and gents attended the opening yesterday afternoon and a most enjoyable time was spent. The bright and well lit appearance of the hall was much praised and in good condition. Quite 60 used the skates, the majority of skaters being adept who had learned proficiency at Plymouth's first rink.

There was a large attendance in the evening when the hall, being lit by a SUNLIGHT burner, looked very gay and animated. On both occasions the band, under Mr J.C. Fly, occupied the platform and discoursed sweet music …

Although situated some distance from many parts of Plymouth the Albert Hall is most centrally situated for The Three Towns and is near to Stoke which sends a large contingent. The opening certainly was auspicious.

The rink at Eldad proved very popular, especially with young ladies, as this report, by 'Non Skater', from the *Western Daily Mercury* of 23rd November 1875 testifies:

Certainly, the Albert Hall, Plymouth, now presents a very animated appearance on a fine afternoon, with its crowd of busy skaters, and the outer fringe of friends and parents come to see the sport.

On Saturday there were nearly 140 on the rink at one time, the majority of whom were young ladies. So far as my experience goes, the art of skating consists of knowing how to tumble down without hurting oneself; this accomplished, the rest follows as a matter of course.

I noticed that the Plymouth ladies have studied the art of tumbling down gracefully; they lose their centre of gravity in a very superior manner; they roll over each other that you wish to see them do it again.

The enthusiastic Arundell Smith also sought to put local skating on a sound footing by setting up the *Three Towns Skating Rink Society* on December 1st 1875.

Skating, like other forms of entertainment in Britain in the late 19th century, was rapidly becoming a very competitive business. Arundell Smith's lease on the Albert Hall was about to expire by the end of that month and the owner, Thomas Martin, realising the lucrative potential of skating, lost no time in issuing this Press notice in the *Western Daily Mercury* of 16th December 1875:

Yet another postcard in a 'Rinking' series, this one published by the Philco Publishing Co. is No. 4107. The card was sent from Truro to North Hill, Launceston, March 1910, with the message 'don't you fancy your self, eh.'.

Albert Hall Skating Rink, Plymouth:
At the expiration of Mr A Smith's lease of the above building
It will be converted into one of the
LARGEST RINKS IN THE WEST OF ENGLAND
And at lower terms of subscription and admission than charged
At any other Rink in the neighbourhood
THOS. S. MARTIN, Proprietor

Thomas Martin, Manager of the Devon & Cornwall Skating Rink Company,[11] – who already ran a successful skating rink at Torquay, and later another at Northernhay, Exeter - closed the Albert Hall temporarily for new flooring, reopening the refurbished building at 3pm on 14th February, 1876.

Thomas Martin closed his Albert Hall rink for the summer months. This was quite usual as most indoor skating sessions took place in the colder months, from late September until late March. Rink proprietors could then use the opportunity of a summer break to refurbish their rinks.

By the summer of 1876 Thomas Martin was looking for a new lessee to manage the Albert Hall rink as Arundell Smith's interests clearly lay elsewhere. An advertisement in the *Western Daily Mercury* that August stated *'The Albert Hall to let'*.

However, it appears that Martin eventually decided not to lease it to another manager but would manage the rink himself, hiring exhibition skaters and other novelty acts to attract patrons to his Albert Hall.[12]

In September 1878 his advertisement for a lady walker appeared:

This day starting at every hour tonight
The greatest walking feat on record
MADAME BLANCHE VICTOR
The Champion Lady Pedestrienne of the World
And recipient of the Championship Gold Medal
Who recently accomplished the extraordinary feat of
Walking 1000 quarter miles in 1000 consecutive
Periods of 10 minutes will, previous to her departure for Paris
WALK 1,800 miles in 1000 consecutive hours
Starting at the floor day and night and
Walking a mile and a half each time
Until she has completed 1,800 miles
Skating as usual [13]

Another advertisement in the *Western Daily Mercury* of 28th October 1878 announced *'A Grand Fancy Dress Skating Assembly and Dance without*

Skates' but also revealed that part of the hall was partitioned off for tennis, another recent sporting craze. The Albert Hall rink remained a popular skating venue for several years, the managers putting on many kinds of entertainment to woo clients.[14]

THE MECHANICS INSTITUTE, DEVONPORT

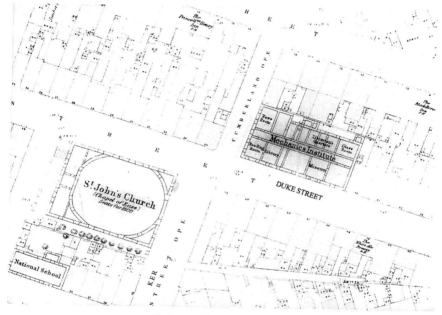

Ordnance Survey Map, 1893

At the end of 1875 yet another rink, the third in The Three Towns, opened on the 16th December. The Brighton Roller Skating Co. was to provide skating facilities at The Mechanic's Institute, Devonport, and the new venue was duly opened by the Mayor.

Established in 1825 the Institute provided a wide range of social, educational and cultural activities. However, it did not acquire its own purpose-built premises in Duke Street until 1843 when a handsome building was erected at a cost of £1,400. There were class and committee rooms, a chess room, and a large news room. On the ground floor were four spacious rooms, totalling some 86 feet in length and divided by broad archways, that were to be used as the museum and library.

In 1849 an extension was added in the same Italianate style. It included a large lecture hall which could hold 1100 persons. This large and magnificent room measured 61 feet by 46 feet wide and was over 30 feet in height. Its most outstanding features were a surrounding gallery and a richly decorated ceiling, adorned with a splendid chandelier. This hall, presumably, was where the skating took place.

An advertisement in the *Western Daily Mercury* announced the forthcoming opening of the skating venue:[15]

NEW SKATING RINK.

THE BRIGHTON ROLLER SKATING
COMPANY
WILL OPEN
ON THURSDAY DECEMBER 16TH,
AT THE
MECHANICS' INSTITUTE, DEVONPORT
In the Large Hall.
ALL THE BRIGHTON NEW PATENT SKATES
WILL BE INTRODUCED.

Malcolmson's Patent Steel Keel'd Roller Skates.
Howle's Patent Spring Bar Flying Roller Skate.
Victoria and Albert Patent Roller Revolving Skate.
Goddard's Patent Skate " Belgravia."
Spiller's Patent Regulator Skate.

Also, the above Company will OPEN the
BUCKLAND HALL, PLYMOUTH,
AS A
ROLLER SKATING CLUB AND SCHOOL.

Admission One Shilling, Morning 11 o'clock, Afternoon 3 o'clock. Skates 6d.
Admission, Evening, Half-past Seven o'clock, 6d. Skates 6d

No further reports could be found of the Mechanics Institute rink but it would appear that skating here was short-lived. By 1881 the Institute began to lose money, no longer able to compete with advances in education. The building, with its museum and library, was transferred to Devonport Borough Council, changing hands for £2,500.[16]

By the early 1950s it had fallen into disrepair but was later used as a Vehicle Tax Office. In recent years it was taken over for a short period by the Pot Black Snooker Club but it is now locked and bolted and the whole historic edifice appears to be in a very sorry state.

This three storey building, nos.18-20 Duke Street which is in the Devonport Conservation Area and Grade II listed, is now on Plymouth's *Buildings At Risk Register*. The report states that *'Windows are broken, rotten roof, eaves and rainwater goods in very poor condition, render discoloured and badly cracked.*

It is sad to see such a fine building fall into disrepair.[17]

Nos 18-20 Duke Street, Devonport, the former Mechanics Institute. This photograph, showing the state of disrepair, was taken in August 2007.

THE BUCKLAND HALL, STATION ROAD, PLYMOUTH

The previous advertisement for the Mechanics Institute, dated 16th December 1875, also announced that the Brighton Roller Skating Co. was to open a 'Roller Skating Club and School' at the Buckland Hall, Station Road, Plymouth, together with a Cycling Club. Cycling was another fast-growing craze with the penny-farthing bicycle and was to become even more popular in the late 1880s, especially with the ladies, due to Dunlop's invention of the pneumatic tyre.

Another small advertisement in the *Western Daily Mercury* the following day gave more details:

> *NEW SKATING RINKS – The Brighton Roller Skating Company yesterday opened skating rinks at the Mechanics' Institute, Devonport and the Buckland Hall, Plymouth. The rink at the institute was formally opened by the Mayor of Devonport. During the season*

it is intended by the proprietors to use all the new patent skates that have been brought out, so that the lovers of skating will have their choices of the many clever inventions that are placed at their disposal.

This fourth skating venue, situated between Adelaide Road and Union Street and next to Farley's Hotel, officially opened on 6 January 1876. However, the Buckland Hall did not last long as a rink. The Brighton-based company may have felt that competition from the Albert Hall and the proposed Westwell Street rinks was too strong.

Local directories show that by 1877 part of the hall had become the home of the Presbyterian Sabbath School

and they had taken over the whole of the premises by 1882. At the turn of the century the building was being occupied by Mitchell, Printers.

PLYMOUTH CRICKET GROUND FETE

During these early years of rinkomania in The Three Towns every opportunity was grasped to provide skating facilities. On Easter Monday and Tuesday 1876 a 'skating rink' was set up on Plymouth Cricket Ground. In 1862 Plymouth Cricket Club had moved from a site on the Hoe to Prince Rock, probably where the Astor Playing Fields are today. The advertisement reads:

This day, weather permitting
FETE and GALA on the Cricket Ground
Entrance sixpence New Programme
OPEN AIR SKATING
Athletic Sport Donkey Derby
Oh my! Oh my! Fireworks!
Roland's Grand Concert at eight o'clock
At St James Hall

An account of the Easter Monday Fete in the *Western Daily Mercury* appeared the next day on another page and reported that of all the entertainments this open air rink was 'the greatest attraction and caused much merriment'.[18]

THE WESTWELL STREET RINKS

By the end of 1875 it was clear that the popularity of 'rinkomania' was firmly established in The Three Towns. The huge public demand for bigger and better rinks – and not least, the money that could be made from them – encouraged entrepreneurs to provide more skating facilities. The Albert Hall's former lessee/manager, Arundell Smith, decided to build his own hall primarily to include a skating rink. In December 1875 it was announced in the Press that he was issuing:

> '...a prospectus inviting subscriptions to the Three Towns' Skating Rink Society, the subscribed capital to be employed in building a large skating rink on the vacant vicarage ground opposite the Guildhall in Westwell Street.

The financial requirements of this scheme, typical of many nation-wide enterprises of this period, had been carefully drawn up:

> '... it has not been thought desirable at the present by the promoter to form a limited liability company, but to float the concern of raising money on the security of the property, after the costs of building it have been defrayed. The subscriptions are therefore to take the form of mortgage debentures on the land and buildings, which will bear interest at 5% and will be repaid at 50% premium or £15 for each £10 subscription.

> £5,000 is the capital required and as no-one knows better than Mr Smith how a large rink should succeed in Plymouth his assertion that the net profits of the undertaking would be not less than £1,000 per annum ought to render it an easy matter to raise the amount necessary.

> The promoter, or 'proprietor' as he is named in the prospectus, would pay off the subscribed capital by annual drawings and when the whole liability had been removed the property would be his own. Meanwhile he would receive £6 per week as his salary. Such is the proposal he puts before the public ...'[19]

The construction of this building on a site once belonging to the vicarage, to be named the *St Andrew's Hall*, duly commenced and continued throughout 1876.

The Westwell Street Open Air Rink

While the building of his St Andrew's Hall was in progress Arundell Smith decided to provide a temporary open-air rink alongside the site. This was the fifth skating location to be launched in The Three Towns. The area was described as:

'... a public place called Guildhall Square about 100 feet in width between Westwell Street and Catherine Street having the Guildhall and Law Courts on one side and the Council Chambers and Municipal Offices on the other...' [20]

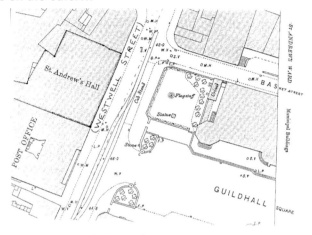

Ordnance Survey Map, 1895

This temporary rink with a 'splendid cement floor' was ready to open on 7th August 1876. There were to be four skating sessions – from 10am-12; 1-3pm; 4-6pm and 7.30-10pm. Shareholders were admitted free and season tickets held by former patrons of the Albert Hall could be used there. Being a mainly winter pursuit, skating outdoors on a summer's evening was something of a novelty and was very well supported as this report shows:

Yesterday evening the new rink in Westwell Street was illuminated with Chinese lanterns and a very pretty effect was produced. There was a large attendance and all the skaters appeared to thoroughly enjoy themselves. Many persons were present who had never been in a rink before and the rapid movements of the crowd of rinkers as they glided around beneath the lanterns appeared to excite great wonder.[21]

St Andrews Church & Guildhall Square, the exact site of the open air skating rink, August 1876. The postcard (no.38G), no publisher shown, was posted in April 1909.

Sadly, all did not go well with the construction of the St Andrew's Hall nearby. On 31st August 1876 an 'accident of a somewhat serious nature occurred', the verdict being that it was 'a wonder it was not attended with a considerable loss of life'.

There had been some delay in the supply of support columns and the builder, a Mr Partridge, not wishing to interrupt building, allowed his men to proceed with the work. During his absence the men struck a centre support and knocked away the 'key' of the wall causing some 50 feet of masonry to fall inwards. Four men were hurt, one needing treatment for head injuries at the Stonehouse and Devonport Hospital.

Some thought the accident had been caused by high winds but others believed that the simple cause was that 'the wall was worked on too rapidly'. However, the incident led to a delay in the opening of the rink at St Andrew's Hall.[22] Furthermore, heavy scaffolding around this proposed skating venue had encroached on part of the open air rink, forcing this temporary rink to close.

Fortunately, Thomas Martin came to the rescue, opening his Albert Hall rink early for skating on 22nd September to ensure that The Three Towns had adequate skating facilities.

St Andrew's Hall Rink, Westwell Street

At last Arundell Smith's long-awaited rink at the St Andrew's Hall, Westwell Street, was ready to open. Built in the Grecian style from designs by J.H. Keats at a cost of £2,000 it was the intention that the hall be used for public gatherings as well as for amusements. It finally opened as *The St Andrews Hall Skating Rink* on Boxing Day 1876 – but still under the umbrella of the Devon & Cornwall Skating Rink Company. The venue also incorporated a 'bicycle school'.[23]

An interesting photograph of the St Andrew's Hall, Westwell Street which shows that it was a very lively place of entertainment.
(Steve Johnson's Cyberheritage *website)*

There were few press reports of skating events at the St Andrew's Hall but this notice did give details of skating times and prices:

The Skating Rink, St Andrew's Hall, Guildhall Square,
opens every day at
11am – 3pm – 7.45pm for two hours each time
The band plays on Mon., Thurs., Sat. afternoons
Admission: Daytime 1/- Children under 14 - 6d. Use of skates 6d.
Packets of tickets and periodical tickets issued at much reduced rates[24]

As was the case at local rinks the most popular events were the skating exhibitions. Skilled executors of the art were regularly booked to amaze and delight the public, the entertainment on a par with music hall and variety acts. On April 19th 1877 star skaters the *Lillywhites* performed there[25] and a few days later, the *Brothers Lane*, 'in their graceful, daring and wonderful evolutions on Plimpton's roller skates', appeared during the last week of April.[26] A glowing report stated that 'the evolutions of the Brothers Lane upon the roller skates borders on the miraculous.'[27]

During that same month a Benefit Night was held for the skating instructor, Mr H.W. Bentley, and in June 1877 it was the turn of the band to have a Benefit Night during which, at 9pm, there would be a 'comic scene by two interlopers'.[28]

The rink also offered other diversions. Cycling was becoming a very popular Victorian pastime and cycling demonstrations were a regular feature of the St Andrews' Hall programme.

The *Ariel penny-farthing bicycle was all the rage in the 1870s until a more modern design with pneumatic tyres was introduced in the 1880s*

Bicycle Evolutions!
By riders in fancy costumes
The GIANT 'Ariel' Bicycle
will positively be ridden
as well as the 'Dwarf' Bicycle
and the NEW Coventry BICYCLE
Band and skating as usual[29]

There was also a *'Pedestrian Walking Feat'*, or *'Marathon'*, with valuable prizes at a *'Grand Athletic Sports'* in 1880.[30]

In 1881 a new, improved skating floor was installed and skating contests held, again on the Plimpton skates. Furthermore, part of the hall was partitioned off occasionally for tennis.[31]

For a short while in the summer of 1878 the hall was used as a temporary theatre while the Theatre Royal was being refurbished after a serious fire. William White's *History, Gazeteer & Directory of the County of Devon, 1878-79* explained that: *'During the reconstruction of the Theatre Royal the skating rink has been fitted with a stage, scenery, etc. and is successfully used as a theatre'.*

The last two managers of the St Andrew's Hall were Thomas Martin and a Mr George Moon who succeeded him.

By 1884 the St Andrew's Hall was put up for sale. The purchaser, a Dr C.A. Hingston of Sussex Terrace, paid £4,750 for the building. However, it was reported that: 'within half an hour of purchase a well-known building contractor of the west of England offered £5,000 and was very disappointed to find it had already changed hands.'[32]

The St Andrew's Hall was later to be incorporated into the new Post Office building, the foundation stone for which was laid by Mr P S Macliver, a former Member of Parliament for Plymouth. Designed by Mr E G Rivers of Bristol, a surveyor to HM Commissioner of Works, it was constructed

10,642—5   GENERAL POST OFFICE. PLYMOUTH.   ROTARY PHOTO. E.C.

The St Andrews Hall was later to be incorporated into the GPO building centre seen here on this pre-1918 Rotary Photo postcard (No.10.642-5)

of Portland stone and Cornish granite in the Gothic style. The contractor
was Messrs Lapthorn and Goad of Plymouth and the cost of the site and
building amounted to £16,500.[33]

PAVILION NEW SKATING RINK

During the time that the St Andrew's Hall rink at Westwell Street was
being constructed the sixth rink of The Three Towns had opened in Martin
Street, The Octagon, very near to the St James Hall. (The St Andrew's
Hall completion brought the rink total to seven.)

CIRCUS ROYAL,

MARTIN STREET, PLYMOUTH,

(By Permission of the Worshipful the Mayor,)

WILL OPEN on MONDAY, December 12th,
1859, for the Winter Season, by the Allied Troupe of
Male and Female Artistes, consisting of the most eminent
members of the Profession.

GREAT FEATS OF GYMNASIA.
THE CHAMPION VAULTERS of the 19th CENTURY,
PROFESSORS OF THE CORD OF TENSION.
ACROBATIC WONDERS AND ANTIPODEAN
FEATS EXTRAORDINARY.

The great achievements of this Monster Troupe have
gained for them the title of the STAR COMPANY of the
WORLD.

For details of this Extraordinary Entertainment see Day
Bills.   [1352

The Pavilion New Skating Rink, managed by Messrs. Snawdon & Chislett,
was housed in what was formerly Ginnett's Hippodrome & Circus. There
had been other entertainment venues in Martin Street – the Alhambra
(c.1862), the Circus Royal (1859)[34] and the Temperance Music Halls – but
the new Hippodrome building, which staged its first performance in October
1874, was truly magnificent:

GINNETT'S NEW GRAND MAMMOTH
HIPPODROME and CIRCUS
Martin Street, Octagon, Plymouth
Will open on Monday October 26th
with a splendid stud of fifty horses and fairy ponies
And a first class troupe of Foreign and British artistes

A description of the premises and the spectacular event was contained
in this report:

GINNETT'S CIRCUS – It is now a considerable time since Plymouth was visited by a circus and last night the inhabitants of The Three Towns testified their appreciation of this class of entertainment by crowding the spacious Hippodrome recently erected in Martin Street.

The famous Cirque in the Champs Elysees, Paris, on which Ginnett's Hippodrome & Circus in Martin Street, the Octagon, was modelled.

The Hippodrome is constructed of iron on a new and novel principle, after the model of the celebrated Cirque in the Champs Elysees, Paris. It is 350 feet in circumference and will include magnificent carpeted and cushioned stalls, elegant and beautiful boxes, an enormous promenade 300 feet long glittering with glass candelabras, recherché pictures and statuettes: being the grandest and most agreeable promenade ever erected in the town: the spacious comfortable pits, noble and monster galleries – the whole with ease and comfort will accommodate 2,000 visitors, besides the Cirque of 140 feet and stabling for 50 horses and ponies.

The grand illuminations of the monster building will consist of 350 gas jets and 25 glass chandeliers – the whole erected in a firm, safe and substantial manner at a cost of £700.

Director of the arena   Mr Smith
Business Manager   Mr Vokes
Sole Proprietor   Mr F Ginnett[35]

The Circus proprietor, Mr F Ginnett, had erected a temporary canvas tent at the top of Market Street, Torquay, in 1874 prior to building a permanent circus site in that town in 1886. By the early 1900s his circus was travelling around the West Country as indicated on this Newquay card.

Ginnett's travelling circus appeared twice nightly in Newquay according to this poster displayed in the town's Beach Road. The card, published by Hartnall's of Newquay, was posted from Redruth to Cardiff in January 1906.

In January 1875 Ginnett's Circus welcomed a troupe of Russian skaters to entertain the public. The following advertisement appeared in the *Western Daily Mercury*:

> *'THE RUSSIAN SKATERS now crowding Ginnett's Circus every evening have the honour to announce to the public of Plymouth that they have appeared before the Emperors of Russia and Germany.'*

> *After their first Performance on Tuesday last, Mr Ginnett, the proprietor of the Circus, was so delighted at the novelty, extravagance, audacity, and grace of their Skating that he RE-ENGAGED THEM FOR ANOTHER WEEK. They have much pleasure also in stating that he has placed the Circus in the Afternoons at their disposal; they, therefore, will give LESSONS IN SKATING on the Russian principle, which is easily acquired, from Two o'clock till Six, on the afternoons of January 4th, 5th, 7th and 8th. Admission 1s. each. The Rink will be erected in the ring. Instructions given free. All persons wishing to Skate on the Rink will be charged 6d. per pair of skates per hour.*

THE RUSSIAN SKATERS

NOW CROWDING

GINNETT'S CIRCUS

EVERY EVENING

Have the honour to announce to the public of Plymouth that they have appeared before the

EMPERORS OF RUSSIA AND GERMANY

And, after their first Performance on Tuesday last, Mr. Ginnett, the proprietor of the Circus, was so delighted at the novelty, extravagance, audacity, and grace of their Skating, that he immediately RE-ENGAGED THEM FOR ANOTHER WEEK.

They have much pleasure also in stating that he has placed the Circus in the Afternoons, at their disposal; they, therefore, will give LESSONS in SKATING on the Russian principle, which is easily acquired, from Two o'clock till Six, on the Afternoons of January 4th, 5th, 7th, and 8th.

Admission 1s. each. The Rink will be erected in the ring. Instructions given free. All persons wishing to Skate on the Rink will be charged 6d. per pair of skates per hour.

Following this taster for roller skating the Pavilion New Skating Rink duly opened in Ginnett's premises on 9th October 1876, promising that *'no expense has been spared in making this the largest and most convenient rink in the West of England.'* Like its competitors the Pavilion New Skating Rink booked skilled executors of the skating art to amaze and delight the public, the entertainments on a par with music hall and variety acts. The following exhibition was one of the highlights:

Illustrations of High Class Roller Skating
Will be given by the celebrated American skaters
Mr Charles Moore and Miss Carrie Moore
Monday June 4th 1877
For one week only
Every afternoon at 3.30 and 4.30
Every evening at 8 and 9
Programme for afternoon:
Varsovienne on skates by Carrie Moore
Programme for evening
Scientific skating
Exhibition of one-wheeled skate by C. Moore
And the last two evenings
Comic act of the Growing Giant [36]

[A Varsovienne was a French dance resembling a Polish national dance]

By October 1876 it had added wrestling to its programme – as a spectator attraction of course – and, as did other rinks, it also provided a Bicycle School.

The popularity of the Pavilion New Skating Rink was another short-lived enterprise and it reverted to staging circuses. In January 1880 WG Pinders' Great Continental Circus promised a 'great attraction and budget of fun with Mr Cruikshank, singing clown and skate dancer'.[37]

By 1890 it had become *The People's Palace, the Empire of the West,* and before long was staging only variety & music hall. Its proprietors, the famous Livermore Brothers, were to become wealthy impresarios in the North of England.

Even this arrangement appears to have been short-lived for this 1898 plan shows proposed alterations to the premises for industrial use. One part is clearly marked *'Section thro Jam Factory'* while another area is marked *'Pickle Factory'*, and there is also *'Space for Waggons'*.

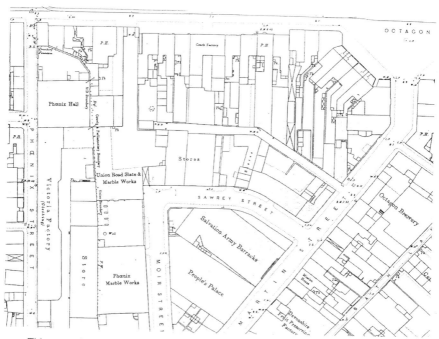

This map shows the locations of both the 'People's Palace' and the 'Phoenix Hall'
Ordnance Survey Map, 1895

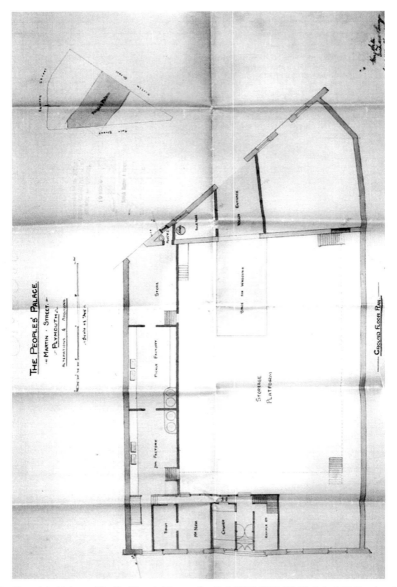

The People's Palace, Martin Street, Plymouth Ref: PCC/60/1/6042 dated 13 September 1898. Plans and associated building notice showing proposed alterations and additions to premises floor plans, elevations, sections and block plan of site.
Architect: King and Lister. Owner: Mr Nash. Application approved, 19 September 1898.
(West Devon Record Office)

PHOENIX HALL RINK, PHOENIX STREET, STONEHOUSE

One of the last of the nineteenth century skating rinks - the Phoenix Hall Rink in Phoenix Street - opened in May 1880. This eighth Victorian rink was managed by a Mr Weston who had once been in charge of skating at the St Andrew's Hall. Situated not far from the Pavilion New Skating Rink it was a popular venue while it lasted and, like other rinks, brought in star skaters to entertain the clientele, a *Monsieur Crowther, the 'King of Skaters'* appearing there in October 1881.

The hall was still being used for skating in 1885 according to the local *Eyres Bros. Directory*.[38] However, though it was still listed as a rink in their 1893 directory it no longer advertised skating.

The building was also known as the *Phoenix Hall of Amusements* and housed the *Fancy Fair,* an entertainment park with amusements which were frowned on by many moral guardians of The Three Towns. They criticised them as 'objectionable and low in tone' and they also considered 'juvenile depravity' to be a problem. In 1886 the tenant, a Mr Wallser, was given notice to quit, critics believing that this would surely be a blessing to the 'long-suffering' inhabitants of Phoenix Street. This place of recreation could then be used for 'a more respectable purpose.'

An editorial in *The Western Figaro* entitled *Shutting Up of the Fancy Fair* states that it does not believe closing the place will bring about any moral change. It makes very interesting reading!

> All at once and acting upon a sudden impulse, Messrs. Baxendale, who are the modern representatives of the ancient firm of Pickford & Co. have resolved to shut up the Fancy Fair in Phoenix Street. That is they have come to the conclusion to give the present tenant Mr Wallser notice to clear out, and when the shooting galleries, and whirligigs and Aunt Sallies and the rest of the playthings in the delightful place of entertainment are removed, then the ground will be utilised for some other and more respectable purpose.
>
> Perhaps another mission hall will be started there, as the mission business seems to be exceptionally popular right now; or at any rate the Messrs. Baxendale no doubt see some way to making their premises as remunerative as they are under the present circumstances. We shall however get rid of the objectionable Fancy Fair and we generally fear that a worthy band of reformers, who had made it the business of their existence to abolish the nuisance will find their occupation, like Othello's, gone.

Now the question will come – will the abolition of the Fair effect the moral reform of the region; will certain well-meaning folk hope and believe? With all respect to them, we have no faith that it will. The Fancy Fair is doubtless a place of assignation, having a round of amusements we are utterly unable to comprehend; but there are other places that are equally places of assignation: the Pier, the Hoe, the Theatre; nay the mission halls, Churches and Chapels are places of assignation, unless people go about with their eyes comfortably closed to existing facts.

Granted the Fancy Fair is decidedly low in tone, and its removal will be a blessing to the respectable inhabitants of the region of Phoenix Street; but the moral regeneration that its closing is to effect will not, in our opinion, spread much further than the contiguous publics. No one will be sorry for the closing of this place of recreation, except for those who immediately or indirectly profit by it, but it is idle to imagine that with its disappearance we get rid of any very considerable element in the question of juvenile depravity.

The question can only be dealt with by the re-enactment of laws which it was the summit of folly ever to abolish; and we say boldly that a large portion of the philanthropic and amiable person whose clamour has resulted in the shutting up of this place are the very ones that have materially helped to obtain the suspension of the laws to which they allude. What they have done in the cause of morality on the one hand has been out-weighed a dozen times over, by the mischief they have effected with the other. They are trying to drip this ocean dry with a colander.[39]

The Phoenix Hall and its so-called vices was eventually demolished to be replaced in 1893 by the splendid *New Palace Theatre*. It was here in 1918 that a specialty skating act, *Billy and Burke*, was engaged to appear on the music hall bill for which they were paid the princely sum of £15.[40]

CHAPTER FIVE

THE DECLINE OF RINKOMANIA

One by one the Victorian rinks of The Three Towns closed down. All had proved to be a short-term investment and only one venue continued to hold roller skating sessions – the Plymouth Pier.

PLYMOUTH PIER

Right at the end of the 19th century the ninth and last Victorian skating venue was provided. Plymouth Pier, a grand and innovative structure built by the Corporation at a cost of £45,000, opened in May 1884.

Five years later 5000 shares at £1 each were issued to finance the building of a large, circular steel pavilion with a glass roof.

The Pier Pavilion was a very lively place of entertainment where orchestral concerts, dancing, wrestling contests, and boxing tournaments took place. Plymouth Pier introduced a roller rink in the Pavilion in the 1890s and enthusiasts could always practice their sport here during winter months long after the other venues had closed. Skating at this popular venue continued almost up to the start of World War Two and was the only rink operating in both the Victorian and Edwardian eras.

Plymouth Pier.

The DIRECTORS of the PLYMOUTH PIER COMPANY request
the honour of your presence on the occasion of

THE OPENING CEREMONY,
BY
THE RIGHT WORSHIPFUL THE MAYOR,
(JOHN GREENWAY, Esq.)
On THURSDAY, MAY 29th, 1884.

Guests are requested to be in their Seats by 2.30 p.m.
EDWARD S. LANCASTER,
Hon. Sec.

This Card will admit Two.
[OVER.

An unusual close-up of the entrance to Plymouth Pier.
Mary writes to her friend in Penzance: I went up here last night.
If you want a change that's the place to go, enjoying myself fine.
The pre-1918 card was published locally by Albert Pengelly.

A later view of Plymouth Pier with a battleship in the background. The card by an unknown
publisher was posted from Looe to Exmouth in July 1938.

The interior of the Plymouth Pier Pavilion on a postcard sent from Devonport to Mutley on 6 September 1907. No publisher is shown but the card is numbered 510 and 70302.
(Graham Brooks collection)

In January 1900 during the winter skating season two daily sessions were held – from 11am to 12.45pm and from 3pm until 4.45pm. A shorter evening period for roller skating took place from 7.45 to 8.30pm. Skating continued well into the Edwardian era as these programmes show.

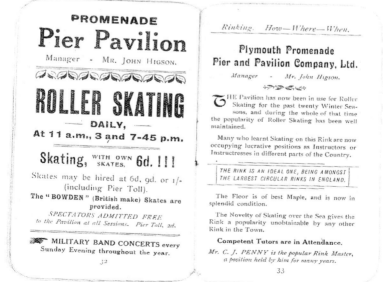

PROMENADE
Pier Pavilion
Manager - MR. JOHN HIGSON.

ROLLER SKATING
—— DAILY, ——
At 11 a.m, 3 and 7-45 p.m.

Skating, WITH OWN SKATES. 6d. !!!

Skates may be hired at 6d, 9d. or 1/-
(including Pier Toll).
The "BOWDEN" (British make) Skates are provided.
SPECTATORS ADMITTED FREE
to the Pavilion at all Sessions. Pier Toll, 2d.

☞ MILITARY BAND CONCERTS every Sunday Evening throughout the year.

32

Rinking. How—Where—When.

Plymouth Promenade
Pier and Pavilion Company, Ltd.

Manager - Mr. John Higson.

THE Pavilion has now been in use for Roller Skating for the past twenty Winter Seasons, and during the whole of that time the popularity of Roller Skating has been well maintained.

Many who learnt Skating on this Rink are now occupying lucrative positions as Instructors or Instructresses in different parts of the Country.

THE RINK IS AN IDEAL ONE, BEING AMONGST THE LARGEST CIRCULAR RINKS IN ENGLAND.

The Floor is of best Maple, and is now in splendid condition.

The Novelty of Skating over the Sea gives the Rink a popularity unobtainable by any other Rink in the Town.

Competent Tutors are in Attendance.

Mr. C. J. PENNY is the popular Rink Master, a position held by him for many years.

33

Pier Pavilion, Plymouth

MANAGER — — — MR. JOHN HIGSON.

ROLLER SKATING

The Pavilion Roller Skating Rink has been specially prepared and is open

EVERY WEEK DAY

Mornings, 11 to 12-45.
Afternoons, 3 to 4-45.
Evenings, 7-45 to 9-30.

SEASON TICKETS :

To include Skating (with own Skates), Carnivals, and Sunday Evening Concerts are now obtainable, price **15s.** Skating only **10s.**

Half-price to children under 13 years of age. Book of 12 tickets, 3s.

SKATES MAY BE HIRED.

Plimptons 6d. Extensions 9d. Ball-bearings 1s.
(including admission to the Pier)

Use of floor for owners of Skates 6d. (including admission).

Grand Military Promenade Concert

EVERY SUNDAY EVENING at 8 o'clock.

Griffiths & Son, Printers, 83 Cambridge Street, Plymouth.

Promenade Pier Pavilion

MANAGER ... MR JOHN HIGSON.

WEDNESDAY, JANUARY 5th, 1910,

AT 8 P.M.

Grand New Year's Fancy Dress
ROLLER SKATING

CARNIVAL

CONFETTI FETE AND DANCE.

BAND OF THE DEVON R.G.A. (T.F.)

By kind permission of Col. E. B. Jenne, will be in attendance under the direction of Mr. George Miller

Six Prizes will be given to Ladies and Gentlemen appearing in the best Advertisement Costumes.

Two value 10s. Two value 10s. Two value 5s.

Open Amateur Handicap Race

(MILE-AND-HALF.) Prizes value 20s., 10s., and 5s.

½-MILE NOVICE RACE

Prizes value 7s. 6d. and 5s.

The above races will be run under the National Skating Association Rules.

HOCKEY MATCH & TUG-OF-WAR

Plymouth Skating Club versus Outside Teams.

Tickets, admitting skaters to the rink in fancy costume, may be had free of charge.

Confetti will be on sale in the Pavilion and Balcony

Admission—Pier Toll 2d., Pavilion 6d., Balcony 1s

Doors open 7-45. Commence at 8. Carriages at 11.

Griffiths & Son, Printers, Cambridge Street, Plymouth.

Pier Pavilion, Plymouth.

Manager - Mr. JOHN HIGSON.

WEDNESDAY, NOVEMBER 24th, 1909

THE FIRST GRAND

Fancy ÷ Dress ÷ Skating ÷ Carnival,

CONFETTI FETE AND DANCE

FOR THE SEASON

BAND OF THE DEVON R.G.A. (T.F.) (By kind permission of Col. E. B. Jenne)

Will be in attendance, under the direction of Mr. George Miller.

PROGRAMME.

8-0—Entry of Skaters.

8-20—Half-Mile Novice Race.

(12 laps.) 1st prize value 7s. 6d., 2nd value 5s. Entries.

1 B. Evans	4 C. Bassett	7 W. Jordan
2 B. Parsons	5 C. Delafield	8 W. Job
3 G. Gemmett	6 A. Delafield	9 J. Smith
		10 J. Fishley

8-50 Procession of Skaters

and Judging of Costumes, by six disinterested persons who will be selected from the audience.

For the Most Original Costumes worn by Ladies:
1st prize value 20s., 2nd value 10s., 3rd value 5s.

For the Most Original Costumes worn by Gentlemen:
1st prize value 20s., 2nd value 10s., 3rd value 5s.

9-15—1½ Mile Open Amateur Handicap Race.

(36 laps.) 1st prize value 20s., 2nd value 10s., 3rd value 5s. Entries.

1 B. Evans	6 G. Gemmett	11 W. Boon	16 F. Collyer
2 J. Baker	7 C. Sweett	12 G. Stephens	17 W. Jordan
3 A. Batchelor	8 C. Bassett	13 H. Byatt	18 G. Laythorne
4 C. Briggs	9 S. Jane	14 B. Fox	19 J. Fishley
5 G. Hayes	10 P. Ballinst	15 C. Delafield	

9-30—Football Match on Skates

Reds versus Blues.

Reds (Goal, S. Fox. Back, H. Dicks (Capt.) Forwards, J. Baker, A. Batchelor, S. Lethbridge.

Blues (Goal, B. Evans. Back C. Briggs. Forwards, P. Sweett, G. Hayes (Capt.) S. Jane.

NOTE.—Confetti must not be made use of before 9-30, and will be supplied free to skaters, and may be purchased by the general public at 2d. per bag to the pavilion and balcony. Confetti once thrown should not be taken from the floor and used again, as, in consequence of the accumulation of dirt or dust, it is dangerous to do so.

There were probably several reasons why 'rinkomania' died out by the end of the 19th century but some commentators had always warned that the craze might be short lived. The contemporary critic JA Harwood in his 1878 book *'Rinks and Rollers'* questions on the very first page when the demise of rinking might take place:

How long will this craze for rinking last, everyone is asking, to which the reply generally is, except from rink owners, 'Oh, it will soon wear itself out.' For my part, I doubt that it will die away so rapidly, and that rinking is destined to take a permanent place among the institutions of civilized society. However, he grudgingly admits: *'But probably there will be some abatement in the present fever in a short time ... these violent beginnings have violent ends'.*[1]

The craze for rinking in The Three Towns did appear to die down somewhat in the late 1880s. The *Oxford English Dictionary* under the entry for 'rinking' gives a quote from *The Graphic* of January 1885: *'Men since rinking collapsed have 'gone in' more for football'*[2] signifying a change to mass spectator sport rather than mass participation in a leisure activity. Perhaps this, as well as the growing popularity of music hall and variety, goes some way towards explaining the decline of skating in the late nineteenth century.

An interesting but critical article appeared in the 1888 issue of *Doidges Annual*, a Plymouth publication. Under the heading *'Crazed about Skating Rinks'* it commented:

One of the most extraordinary manias of modern times was what was known as the rinking mania. It was a species of madness. A person is revolved round and round on a pair of wheeled skates, which gave him or her the appearance of having club feet, to the discordant sounds of a bad band. This was rinking. And the monotony was only diversified when the person fell with violence on the end of his nose, and broke that feature of his face, or sprained his wrist, or had to be conveyed home in a cab, suffering from concussion of the brain.

Such as it was, however, all classes were for a time quite demented on the subject of rinking. They imagined that they could rink without weariness of satiety for three hundred and sixty-five days of the year. Age would not wither, nor custom stale its infinite variety.

Rinks were constructed in all parts of London, and in most of our country towns; and then, all at once, rinking vanished from the number of popular amusements.[3]

However, the demise of nineteenth century 'rinkomania' did not last long for at the beginning of the twentieth century, even though the Plymouth Pier continued to offer skating facilities, The Three Towns was to be hit by yet another wave of roller skating hysteria even more lively than before!

Promenade Pier Pavilion,

MANAGER — Mr JOHN HIGSON.

Wednesday, March 31st, 1909.

THE LAST GRAND

Fancy Dress Skating Carnival

And CONFETTI FETE for the Season.

BAND of the DEVON R.G.A., (T.F.)

(By kind permission of Col. E. B. Jeune) will be in attendance under the direction of Mr. George Miller.

PROGRAMME.

8-0—Entry of Skaters in Fancy Dress.

8-10—One mile Scratch Race, (24 laps).
Winners of Handicap Races barred. 1st prize value 15s., 2nd value 7/6 Entries :
1 S. Jane   4 F. Collier   7 G. Furguson   10 W. Jordan   13 T. Gidley
2 H. Evett   5 A.W. Brown   8 G. Stephens   11 R. Lillicrap 14 S. Duke
3 A. Batchelor   6 F. Ballisat   9 B. J. Evans   12 A. Brown   15 G.Lapthorn

8-30—Football Match on PIER STAFF v. SKATES. MR. S. CURTIS'S TEAM.
PIER STAFF (Red)—Goal, J. Organ   Back, F. Pollard.   Forwards, J. Cudlip,
S. Cudlip and O. J. Penney.
Mr. CURTIS'S TEAM (Blue)—Goal, S. Fox.   Back, G. Lapthorn.   Forwards,
G. A. Penney, S. Curtis, R. Lillicrap.

9-0—½-mile Novelty Candle Race (12 laps).
Each competitor will be required to wear a night cap and night shirt.
1st prize value 10/-, 2nd value 5s.   Entries—
1 S. Fox   6 A.W. Brown   11 H. Williams   16 A. Brown   21 F. Cowles
2 S. Jane   7 F. Ballisat   12 R. Lillicrap 17 C. Briggs   22 S.Lethbridge
3 H. Evett   8 G. Furguson   13 T. Gidley   18 W. Job   23 G. Lapthorn
4. A.Batchelor 9 G. Stephens   14 W. Jordan   19 S. Duke   24 W. Richards
5 F. Collier   10 P. Sweet   15 S. Curtis   20 G. Penney

9-10—Procession of Skaters
and Judging of Costumes by six disinterested persons, who will be selected from the audience. For the most Original Costumes worn by Ladies—1st prize value 20s., 2nd value 10s., 3rd value 5s. For the most Original Costumes worn by Gentlemen—1st prize value 20s., 2nd value 10s., 3rd value 5s.

9-30—1½ mile Open Handicap Race, (36 laps).
1st prize value 20s., 2nd value 10s., 3rd value 5s.   Entries—
1 S. Fox   5 F. Collier   9 P. Sweet   12 S. Curtis   15 S. Duke
2 S. Jane   6 A.W. Brown   10 W. Jordan   13 S. Cudlip   16 G. Penney
3 H. Evett   7 F. Ballisat   11 A. Brown   14 C. Briggs   17 G. Lapthorn
4 A.Batchelor   8 G. Stephens

9-40—Battle of Confetti.

9-45—The Maxwell Brothers,
the Modern Athletes, present a new, novel and refined act of herculean strength.

10-10—Hockey Match on Skates,
Pier Staff v. Mr. S. Curtis's Team
PIER STAFF (Red)—Goal, F. Pollard.   Back, O. J. Penney.   Forwards, J. Cudlip,
J. Organ, and S. Cudlip.
Mr. CURTIS'S TEAM (Blue)—Goal, A. Brown.   Back, R. Lillicrap.   Forwards, G. A.
Penney, S. Curtis, G. Lapthorn.

NOTE—Confetti must not be made use of before 9-40, and will be supplied free to skaters, and may be purchased by the general public at 2d per bag in the pavilion and balcony Confetti once thrown should not be taken from the floor and used again, as, in consequence of the accumulation of dirt or dust, it is dangerous to do so.

GRAND OPENING OF CONCERT SEASON, 1909.
Good-Friday, Saturday, and Easter Sunday. Special engagement of the Cardiff Military Band, prize winners Welsh National Eisteddfod, 1897 and 1899. (Patron, The Marquis of Bute). Conductor, Mr. J. Matthews. Vocalist, Mr. Trevor Evans, Tenor, who has had the honour of singing before Their Majesties, The King and Queen on several occasions.

Griffiths & Son, Printers, 83, Cambridge Street, Plymouth.

A mint set of six 'Rinking' cards published by Andrew & George Taylor in their 'Orthochrome Series'. Printed in Saxony they are numbered 2830-2835

Published by Shamrock & Co. in their Rinking Revels Series,
this card was sent in December 1911

A Valentine's card sent in January 1913

Chapter Seven:

The Rinking Craze 1909 to 1939

In 1909 The Three Towns, like many other parts of the country, was hit by another skating craze which this time around was known as 'Rinking'. It is not clear why roller skating should have become so popular again in the Edwardian years after its demise in the late 19th century. One minute only a few enthusiasts were skating, the next everyone wanted to indulge.

The popularity of various amusements often came in cycles, for example conkers, hula hoops, marbles, whips and tops and yo-yos, but they could stop as abruptly as they started. So it remains something of a mystery as to why roller skating took off again in the UK in 1909.

A large rink in Chicago had opened in 1902 followed by another in Madison Square Gardens, New York, in 1908. These American enterprises appear to have gone some way towards generating renewed interest in the sport and hundreds more rink openings followed in the United States and Europe.

Rinking. How—Where—When.

A FEW HINTS on this Popular and Fascinating Pastime.

By 1910 there were 526 roller skating rinks in Britain. Bournemouth had four rinks and Birmingham boasted six. Some Edwardian rinks catered for thousands of skaters and spectators and others accommodated just hundreds.[1]

This booklet on Rinking, published in Plymouth in 1910, suggests it may have been the attraction of well-furbished rinks and lively events which made the sport popular again and all credit to the rink proprietors who ensured that their establishments were first class and, above all, fun.

To set the scene for rinking in The Three Towns the booklet article is reproduced here in full:

The past year has witnessed the rise of a new National sport, which has leapt into favour with every class of society, and there can be no doubt whatever that Skating Rinks are supplying a long-felt want, and that Rinking, together with what may be termed the ramifications of Rinking, has come to form one of the permanent pastimes of the people.

The idea that Rinking is a passing fad must be banished once and for all, and one has only to pay a visit to any of the Rinks to be convinced of the grip which this exhilarating and pleasant pastime has on the public.

It is a matter for wonder, however, what the crowds of Skaters that are now to be seen on the various Rinks throughout the Country did with themselves prior to the advent of Rinking.

There has been Roller Skating in most parts of the Country for the past twenty-five years, but the rinks were not of the quality and quantity that they are at the present time, and this fact is mainly responsible for the increased patronage which the pastime enjoys and for the enormous success of the Roller Skating movement generally.

The part the promoters have played in this direction should not be forgotten, however, and it must be very gratifying to them to note the measure of success which has attended their efforts. To them must be given the credit for the splendid arrangements that are made for patrons at the various Rinks, which greatly adds to the comfort and enjoyment of the pleasures of Rinking, and will tend to prevent any lapse from the devotion of the public to the sport.

The growth of these Palaces of Roller Skating is unique in itself, and they may be considered an addition to the attractiveness of any locality. Each has its own particular scheme of decoration, and is provided with a refreshment Bar and Cloak-room accommodation. The Skating Surfaces are perfect, and there is an adequate supply of ball-bearing Skates. The comfort of the spectator has not been overlooked, and those who are responsible have succeeded in providing these patrons with excellent seating accommodation, on raised platforms or balconies, and a full and uninterrupted view of the Skaters.

Rinking as a pastime is exhilarating and fascinating and commends itself to the public as a healthy and physical exercise. It has supplied the need of a sport in which most people, old and young, can actively participate, instead of merely playing the part of spectator, a condition of affairs that exists with most pastimes, and which has been deplored by not a few of our leading professional men.

Even to those who are denied the opportunity, for one reason or another, of enjoying to the fullest extent the pleasure of Skating, the numerous Speed Contests, Carnivals and special occasions that are arranged from time to time by the various managements never fail to provide the onlooker with plenty to interest and amuse.

There can be nothing more exciting than a series of well-organised Races on Roller Skates; nothing more interesting than a clever display of Fancy Skating, and nothing more amusing and entertaining than a well-conducted Fancy Dress Carnival and Confetti Fete of Skaters. These Carnivals are, indeed, a feature, and it is remarkable what a comprehensive range of ideas are usually represented by the competitors. Prizes are offered in connection with these very popular events, and novelties that are calculated to be an attraction frequently introduced.

Fancy or Evening Dress is requested to be worn by Skaters, and, as they move gracefully round to the strains of music, the scene is an animated one in the extreme, with the Grand March Past as a crowning effort. Those with a desire for the spectacular, should not miss seeing these carnivals, and the way they are patronised makes it clear that managers are alive to the necessity of catering for the spectator as well as the performer.

Dancing on Skates has become very popular with both sexes, and nothing is more delightful than waltzing on Rollers, or the more favourite two-step, which is a decided improvement upon, and a welcome relief from, the ordinary round and round variety.

Side by side with those eager for the pleasures of Skating are others with the keenness of competition, and in most of the large centres Rink Hockey is being played to a great extent, and Tournaments are held for both ladies and gentlemen. Looked at in the light of the more vigorous side of this fashionable pastime, the introduction of such an element can only be for its welfare, as it is sure to create enthusiasm and gain favour with the majority. Hockey Leagues are being formed and valuable trophies offered for competition, and there is every indication that, at no distant date, something of a National Competition will develop.[2]

In 1909 large buildings were once more needed in The Three Towns to house the rinks and businessmen were again keen to put their money into roller skating ventures.

A Crop of Croppers at the Plymouth Skating Rink

This standard 'rinking' postcard to which any named location could be added was published by Valentine's. The postmark is unclear but it was sent from Plymouth to A.Rendle, Stoker, HMS Essex, c/o GPO, Devonport, around 1910-11. The message reads: "If I were you I should turn over a new leaf and try rinking instead of drinking or else <u>you will</u> come a cropper. Never mind, cheer up old sport, as long as you don't fall through the door you will be alright. L.C."

Chapter Eight

The Ebrington Street Rink

The first Edwardian rink to open was located in a very large building at 27 Ebrington Street, situated approximately where the Primark store in Drake Circus is now. The massive hall was one of the biggest in Plymouth and measured over 450 feet in length. It was used as a public meeting place as well as for skating.[1]

The new American Roller Skating Rink opened on Friday 17th September 1909 for an invited gathering, with the official opening the next day. The rink, managed by Mr Clemence R Tree, was under the joint directorship of Messrs Crawford and Wilkins who had opened several rinks across Europe and the UK.

Details of the rink together with times of opening as given in the Rinking booklet are shown below:[3]

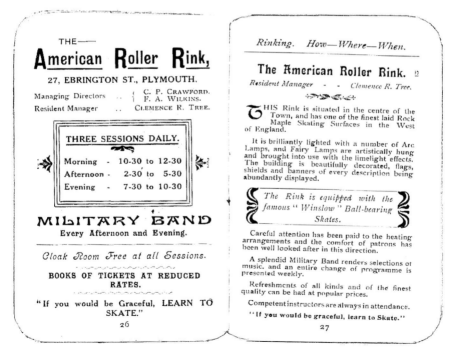

THE——

American Roller Rink,

27, EBRINGTON ST., PLYMOUTH.

Managing Directors .. { C. P. CRAWFORD.
  F. A. WILKINS.
Resident Manager .. CLEMENCE R. TREE.

THREE SESSIONS DAILY.

Morning - 10-30 to 12-30
Afternoon - 2-30 to 5-30
Evening - 7-30 to 10-30

MILITARY BAND
Every Afternoon and Evening.

Cloak Room Free at all Sessions.

BOOKS OF TICKETS AT REDUCED RATES.

"If you would be Graceful, LEARN TO SKATE."

26

Rinking. How—Where—When.

The American Roller Rink. [2]

Resident Manager - - *Clemence R. Tree.*

THIS Rink is situated in the centre of the Town, and has one of the finest laid Rock Maple Skating Surfaces in the West of England.

It is brilliantly lighted with a number of Arc Lamps, and Fairy Lamps are artistically hung and brought into use with the limelight effects. The building is beautifully decorated, flags, shields and banners of every description being abundantly displayed.

The Rink is equipped with the famous " Winslow " Ball-bearing Skates.

Careful attention has been paid to the heating arrangements and the comfort of patrons has been well looked after in this direction.

A splendid Military Band renders selections of music, and an entire change of programme is presented weekly.

Refreshments of all kinds and of the finest quality can be had at popular prices.

Competent instructors are always in attendance.

"If you would be graceful, learn to Skate."

27

*An unusual shot showing the vastness of the empty Ebrington Street rink
on this unused postcard published by Hawkins of Plymouth*

C. P. CRAWFORD ⎱ MANAGING
F. A. WILKINS ⎰ DIRECTORS   **AMERICAN ROLLER RINK CO.**   O. E. LAUMANN,
RESIDENT MANAGER.

*The American Roller Rink Co.'s Hamburg rink, owned by Crawford & Wilkins,
managing directors of their Ebrington Street venture.
This postcard was posted from Hamburg to Glasgow on 13 December 1909*

A daytime session at the Ebrington Street rink on another Hawkins postcard. The message, written on 15 October 1909 reads: Darling, I am sending you this just to give you an idea of our skating rink. This is only a small section of it, it's very large. Ada and I went to the Cinderella last night, it was nice but not a great many there, all the fellows had to wear dress suits, as of course that would keep a lot away. We had a flashlight photo taken of it, so it it's any good when finished I will send you one.

Rinkers in carnival dress line up for another Hawkins photo, the card sent to Hettie from Miss Hilda Hodge

The skating area had been purposely built within the large hall and measured 185 feet by 75 feet having a surrounding promenade, seating space, offices and conveniences together with its own entrance hall. The rink held daily sessions, carnivals, fancy dress evenings, and skating 'Cinderellas' – formal dances with everyone in evening dress. A press report of November 1909 describes the scene perfectly:

> *Patrons daily increase, and the excellence of the floor is a matter of congratulation. The scene in the hall, particularly in the evening, is a brilliant one, the skaters in motion to the accompaniment of the military band, under the flare of the electric light, delighting the spectators. The carnival of last week was remarkably well attended.*[2]

The popularity of the rink seems to have been assured as this Press report shows:

> *The American Roller Skating Rink in Ebrington Street, Plymouth, is becoming quite the most popular institution in the district and Messrs. CP Crawford and FA Wilkins are to be congratulated on the success of their venture. Patrons from The Three Towns, and even distant parts of Devon and Cornwall, attend all three sessions in large numbers, motoring parties coming in from Tavistock, Ivybridge, and other places frequently.*

> *On Saturday afternoon Mr Clemence R Tree, the courteous resident manager, states there were 500 persons on the rink at one time, and even then it was not uncomfortably crowded. The attendants and instructors have strict orders to stop all persons skating above the average pace, and anyone persisting in breaking the rule has to leave the rink.*

> *Skaters find that the military band, under the able direction of Mr P Elford, late of the Royal Marines Band, adds greatly to the pleasure of 'rinking' and helps beginners to keep in step with more experienced pleasure seekers.*[4]

Elegant skating 'Cinderellas' were a regular feature, the first of which was held on 14th October 1909.

American Roller Skating Rink,

Ebrington Street, PLYMOUTH.

MANAGING DIRECTORS - - - - MESSRS. C. P. CRAWFORD AND F. A. WILKINS.

:: :: FIRST GRAND :: ::

SKATING CINDERELLA,

Thursday, Oct. 14th, 1909, 7 to 11 p.m.

American Roller Skating Rink,
Ebrington Street,
Plymouth.

The Management beg to intimate that they have arranged to hold the

:: :: **FIRST** :: :: ::

SKATING CINDERELLA

On Thursday, Oct. 14th, 1909.

As far as attire is concerned, Patrons will be expected to conform to the conventional Evening Dress rule, which secures invariable recognition at Dancing Cinderellas in all polite society. The Ladies will be at perfect liberty to consult their own comfort and convenience in the matter of dispensing with the Court Trains, which, whilst adapted to the Ball Room, are scarcely suitable for Skating.

Masks will neither be required nor permitted.

This Cinderella on Wheels will differ from the modern Cinderella of Terpsichore in only two material respects, viz.:—that Skating will be substituted for dancing, and that the joyous function will close at 11 o'clock instead of the customary later hour associated with the wind-up of dancing Cinderellas.

Skating will begin at 7 o'clock.

The fine Band of the Rink will play appropriate music, and the Hall will be prettily decorated.

Choice Refreshments will be purveyed at the Buffet.

A Uniform Tariff of 1s. per head will be imposed for admission to the Hall, and the Skate Charges for the night will be :—

Lady = =   1s. (or one ticket).
Gentleman =   2s. (or two tickets).
Books of Tickets at reduced rates.

Local newspapers often gave graphic accounts of these events with detailed descriptions of the fashionable dresses worn by the ladies, even naming the wearer. Here is the report of the 'Cinderella' which took place on Thursday 9th December 1909

Roller skating is the favourite pastime of this winter, and every entertainment given at the Ebrington Street Rink only shows more clearly the hold this form of amusement has on our Three Towns public. The 'Cinderella' held there on Thursday evening attracted nearly 350 skaters. And when all these ladies and gentlemen, in evening dress, were gliding round to the strains of the band the spectacle was exceedingly pretty. Coloured limelights thrown on the rink from time to time added to the charm of the scene and, one enthusiast declared, seemed to picture the change from moonlight to dawn.

On Thursday there were many graceful waltzers, and it was a really charming sight to watch them gliding round. The 'Grand March' with its many evolutions, was well carried out, and was immortalised by the inevitable 'flash-light' photographer – a ubiquitous individual without whom no festive gathering is complete.

Hawkins must have made a good income from his skating rink photos. This postcard is of the Cinderella held on 9 December 1909.

93

American Roller Skating Rink,

27, EBRINGTON STREET, PLYMOUTH.

Managing Directors - - - - - - Messrs. C. P. CRAWFORD and F. A. WILKINS.

FIRST SEASON.

GRAND SKATING CINDERELLA,

THURSDAY, DECEMBER 9th, 1909.

The Management have arranged to hold A GRAND SKATING CINDERELLA on THURSDAY Evening, December 9th. Skating will commence at 7 o'clock. All Skaters must be in Evening Dress.

TARIFF
{
Admission to Rink 1/- each (or one ticket).
Skates—Lady 1/- (or one ticket); Gentleman 2/- (or two tickets).
Books of Tickets at Reduced Rates.
}

Copyright No. 36918.

There were eighteen items on the programme, and the music was well rendered by the band, under Mr Elford.

The ladies' fashions were described thus:

All the ladies wore frocks cut short enough for skating, and a large number had elected to wear white. Mrs James Wilson was in shrimp pink silk and cream lace; Mrs Holman Andrews wore a pretty frock of pale pink chiffon and silk; Mrs Clemence Tree (wife of the popular manager) was in pale blue, relieved with cream lace; Mrs Palmer's white gown was cut in princess style; Mrs Aldred's frock of 'broderie Anglaise' was relieved with a touch of red velvet, and she wore red grapes in her hair; Mrs Hellen was wearing white and silver; the Misses Sybil and Violet Thomas (two very graceful skaters) were both in white; Miss Hodgess wore cream silk; Miss Wilkinson in white, with a blue sash; Miss Trevithick wore a charming frock of soft ivory silk, trimmed with lace, and having a deep V of lace on the corsage; and Miss Edith Roberts-Osborn was in white silk and guipure lace, with touches of pale blue velvet.[5]

The festivities were captured by local photographer, Hawkins, and quickly printed as postcards to be sold off to skaters and their families.

Hawkins took the photograph at Ebrington Street for this unused postcard. Written on the reverse is: "This is the Floor Manager and Lady Instructress in the Skating Rink"

March 17 1910 was the date of this Carnival. The Hawkins postcard, showing young and old in a variety of costumes, was sent from Plymouth to a Miss A Jones at Heligan Mill Farm, Mevagissey, in May 1910.

This postcard is embossed on the bottom left-hand corner 'Flashlight, Hawkins, Plymouth'. The photographer has captured a few of the revellers at the Cinderella on 20th April 1910. The card was sent from Plymouth to Southampton on May 3rd 1910.
Maude's message reads: I thought that you might like to have a photo of the 'Cinderella' we had at the skating rink on the 20th. I did not partake in it but only watched but you will notice May and Winnie standing in the front. This photo doesn't include all the skaters because they could not all be taken on a P.C. I think I am coming to Southampton to live soon, probably in June. If there are any photos of the Cinderellas held at S'oton any time will you send me one especially if there is anyone on it.

Crispin Gill remembers Eady as *'a flamboyant showman who interspersed films with live acts on stage. One performer was his well-built daughter, Dorothy, who sang soprano to the accompaniment of a 15-piece orchestra.'* [11]

The two projectionists, BJ Cattell and R Thomas, had transferred to the New Palladium when the Plymouth Picture House in George Street had closed. Their job was not an easy one as binoculars were needed to focus on the screen 150 yards away and they and the film-going audience had to contend with deafening noise when rain beat down on the corrugated iron roof! [12]

The Palladium acquired a large organ from the Church of St Peter in Croydon, the first picture house in Plymouth to have such an instrument. In 1920 it was also the first in the city to demonstrate the new 'Optrics' system of 3D and the cinema was also used as a base in the days of early radio, transmitting under the call sign 5PY.

The cinema was purchased by Denham Picture Houses around 1927 and on 1st November 1929 the first sound film in Plymouth was shown there with a screening of *'The Desert Song'*. Bert Cattell remained as the last projectionist and, like so many other Plymouth buildings, it fell victim to the German bombing of 1941. [13]

Between 1963 and 1965 much of the western end of Ebrington Street was carved up to make way for the Charles Church roundabout and the multi-storey car park. In 1968 that part of the street from Drake Circus was renamed 'Eastlake Street' after Sir Charles Eastlake, the eminent Plymouth judge. The shell of Charles Church now remains as a memorial to the courage of Plymothians during the Blitz.

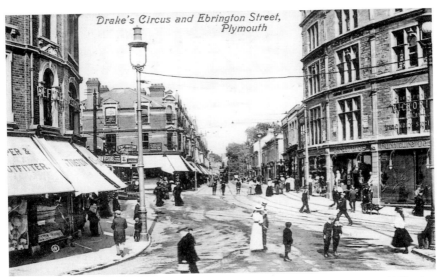

A busy scene at the junction of Drake Circus and Ebrington Street in the early 1900s. In the far distance at the end of Ebrington Street is Charles Church. For almost four decades from the early 1960s the former C&A store, Tesco and the multi-storey car park replaced the shops on the left before even these were demolished to make way for the new Drake Circus shopping mall. This unused postcard was published in the Valentine's Series.

CHAPTER NINE

MILLBAY RINKERIES

Shortly after the opening of the Ebrington Street Rink another skating venue, destined to be the most popular in Plymouth's roller skating history, was being set up. Plans were afoot in September 1909 to make Millbay Rinkeries the largest and most lively rink outside London.

A national company, Rinkeries (1909) Ltd. which controlled Olympia in London, had acquired part of the former four-storied structure, Millbay Soap Works, in Millbay Road. A Soap Manufactory had been established there in 1818 by Thomas Gill and the building had been extended in 1830 to become the Millbay Soap, Alkali & Soda Works. It was later known as just Millbay Soap Works and further extensions were added in 1867. *Millbay Soap* became a household name, the factory capable of producing over 20 tons of soap per hour.

In 1908 the business was bought out by the New Patent Candle Company and *Millbay Soap* manufacture was transferred to their works at Coxside before Lever Brothers acquired the *Millbay* name in 1913.

The skating rink was to be set up in the soap works' old boiler room and packing house. These basement premises, reached by a grand staircase, had their entrance in West Hoe Road.

On 7th October 1909 the Magistrates convened at Plymouth Police Court before the Mayor, Mr AE Spender, Alderman Sir Charles H Radford, Messrs. S Edgcumbe, WS Spear, R Clark and HH Shanks. A Press report gave this summary of the proceedings:

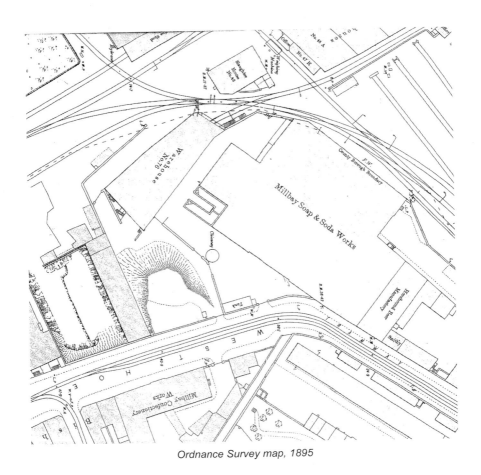

Ordnance Survey map, 1895

MR FW Murray (Watts, Ward & Anthony) applied on behalf of the Chairman and Managing Director of Rinkeries Ltd. for a dancing, singing and music licence for the Plymouth Rinkeries, West Hoe Road, of which Mr John Brock is the local manager.

Mr Murray explained that a company had been formed for the purpose of providing roller skating rinks in the principal towns. The building at Plymouth had an area of over 30,000 feet which enabled the foundation of two rinks, one having an area of 3,400 feet for learners and the other main rink an area of 20,000 feet. In those respects the Rinkeries would compare favourably with any rink in the Kingdom. The plans had been approved by the Borough Surveyor.

It was intended to utilise the building for concerts, bazaars, exhibitions, or entertainments of that kind in the summer time. That, he believed, would meet a long felt want in the town. It was also desired to use the building for band concerts on Sundays, thus enjoying the same privilege as the Promenade Pier. The company had spent £4,000 or £5,000 on the rink, and forty or fifty people would be employed.

Mr SW Haughton, architect and surveyor, having explained the plans he had prepared, the magistrates, after private consultation, granted the license subject to the dancing being "roller skating dancing only", and that on Sundays the concerts consist of only instrumental music.[1]

Millbay Rinkeries began advertising for rink staff even before the magistrates had approved the plans. In September this advertisement appeared:

> WANTED, for MILLBAY RINKERIES, PLYMOUTH.
> Doorkeepers, Ticket Collectors,
> Skating Instructors and Skate Boys
> Preference given to Plymouth residents -
> Apply J Brock, Manager.[2]

A copy of the Rinkeries Ltd employment contract is shown in Appendix X.

A postcard view of the Millbay Rinkeries' impressive entrance in West Hoe Road, by Hawkins of Plymouth.

The opening of Plymouth's second rink was eagerly awaited, one Press report acknowledging that *'the site chosen is an admirable one, being in immediate touch with train and tram service, and for that reason the new rink should instantly attract a large patronage.'*

This same report also congratulated *'the resident manager, Mr Brock, who is well known in Plymouth, and thanks to whose thoughtfulness, local talent will be employed.'*

The Three Towns' skating history was also referred to: *'Plymouth has long possessed some of the finest roller skaters in the country and the work of those engaged will most assuredly be followed, under the circumstances, with more than passing interest.'*

The *Western Independent* was given a preview of the premises and had nothing but praise for the undertaking, describing it as *'a wilderness transformed into a Garden of Paradise'* and that it was *'hardly conceivable that such a huge palace as now exists beneath the grey and grim walls of the old renowned soap works should take the place of a packing room and boiler house.'*

The report went on to describe the exterior and interior of the building, together with the décor and amenities:

> *Abutting on West Hoe Road is an imposing portico by which entrance to the rink is obtained, and as one descends the broad flight of stairs the skate room is on one side, whilst on the other are the refreshments and cloakroom.*

> *On reaching the skating level one gleans an idea of the general decoration of the huge hall, although only a portion of the learners' rink can be seen.*

> *Blended in three rich colours, the walls offer a warm welcome, but it is not until the main rink is reached that the full vista calls for the appreciation of the visitor. A huge expanse of maple wood flooring meets the eye, polished by a powerful electric motor whirling a sand paper belt until the surface scintillates under the rays of the numerous electric lights. These have been installed by Messrs. WJ Corse & Co., and the Osram lamps will shed their brilliancy to the amount of nearly 45,000 candle power, and in addition gas will be used as an illuminant, and also as a medium of heating.*

> *A thousand pairs of famous Richardson skates of all sizes are boxed within the skate room. Simple of construction and built on very similar lines to the original Plimton [sic] skates, these are very much*

lighter than metalled plated rollers. The wheels are grooved in the centre of the running surface, which will permit of a firm holding of the flooring.

Mr AN Coles has completed his task as far as the constructive part of the building is concerned and the maple wood two inch flooring is being laid, under the superintendence of the Company's own foreman, by an army of carpenters and there is very little doubt that the Company's original intention of opening the rink to the public on Wednesday will be realised.[3]

Finally, the long awaited opening day arrived – not the Wednesday, but Thursday, 11th November 1909. During the morning a special session was held so that a large number of ladies and gentlemen could view the building and test the superb maple floor. They were welcomed by the Chairman of Rinkeries (1909) Ltd., and by John Brock, the Manager.

Millbay Rinkeries

WEST HOE ROAD.

One Minute from Millbay Station.

Proprietors · RINKERIES (1909) Ltd
Resident Manager · J. BROCK.

The Chairman and Directors request the presence of Yourself and Friend at the

OPENING

of the

RINKERIES

on

Thursday, November 11th, 1909.

SESSIONS—3.0 to 5 P.M.
7.30 to 10 P.M.

This Card must be given up at the Entrance.

The Learners' Rink at Millbay with manager, John Brock, seated centre front.

In the afternoon hundreds more, both beginners and the more expert, tested out the rink's facilities. However, skating hysteria seems to have heralded the evening session as this report makes clear:

> On the opening night there was a remarkable scene in the Millbay Road, the queue extending nearly to Millbay Station prior to the doors being opened. Inside the vast hall everything was bright and cheerful. Fancy palms graced the entrance, festoons of flags hung on all sides, the myriads of lights were reflected in the polished floor, on which gentlemen and gaily dressed ladies were soon enjoying the bracing exercise, whilst the greater part of the crowd looked on with envy and admiration at the expert evolution and graceful figure skating.

> Everything is being done to carry on the rink as a high class place of recreation, especially for ladies and children. There are two rinks, one for learners and one for the experts, and there are lady and gentlemen instructors in each. These are in uniform and only too anxious to help the novice. It is worth noting that on the opening night, when there were nearly a thousand persons on the rink, there was not a single accident.[4]

The manager, John Brock, sits with the ladies in the Rinkeries' tea room. The notice on the right reads: 'Patrons finding any articles on the Rink kindly return same to Manager immediately.' *The posters on the rear screens state* 'Books of 60 tickets 30/-'
(Hawkins, Plymouth)

MILLBAY RINKERIES,

WEST HOE ROAD, PLYMOUTH.

Resident Manager
J. BROCK.

— ANOTHER —
Grand Novelty Night!

Large Hat and Bow
— Competition —

— ON —
WEDNESDAY, APRIL 26th

A SEASON TICKET is offered for the Lady
wearing what is considered the Best and
Largest Hat and the Gentleman wearing what
is considered the Best and Largest Bow.

NUMEROUS OTHER ATTRACTIONS !
SKATING from 7 to 10-30.

☞ **PRICES AS USUAL.**

Monthly School Children's Tickets 5/-, including Use
of Skates for Mornings and Afternoons.

MITCHELL AND CO., PRINTERS, PLYMOUTH

✄ *Cette Semaine seulement*

A L'

HIPPODROME

American Roller Skating Rink
(PLACE CLICHY)

C. P. CRAWFORD
F. A. WILKINS } Directeurs.

— LA CÉLÈBRE —
FAMILLE GANDY

ENFANTS-ARTISTES
Les mieux payés du Monde
2.000 *francs par semaine.*

MADDE	*ALFRED*	*MABEL*
AGÉE DE 11 ANS	AGE DE 10 ANS	AGE DE 15 ANS
Dans ses gracieuses évolutions.	*Le Patineur le plus merveilleux du monde entier.*	*Artiste finie sur patins.*

Evolutions expertes, artistiques et scientifiques.

EXHIBITIONS MERVEILLEUSES

Tous les Jours { à **4** h. **45** après-midi.
à **10** h. **45** soir.

✄ Changement de Programme à chaque Représentation. ✄

Imp. PONROY & Co., 5, rue Saulnier, Paris

There was a separate area set aside for refreshments and the catering firm providing for skaters and spectators was the well-known local establishment of Genoni's. In December 1911 plans were laid to add massive mirrors to the main hall together with the erection of a gallery with attractive little tea rooms.

Cut out coupons appeared in the Press giving reduced price admission to the Rinkeries to include use of skates: *The admittance coupons appearing in the 'Western Daily Mercury' and the 'Western Evening Herald' have proved a great attraction, no fewer than 500 persons presenting them at the Rinkeries yesterday.*[5]

This practice of offering discount vouchers for local attractions is still a feature of Plymouth newspapers today.

Another ploy Brock used to attract patrons was to offer free admission to the rink – including the use of skates - to the first fifty passing through the turnstiles for the evening session. His slogan was: *'To come early means to skate free'*.

During the first week, to entice yet more patrons, John Brock arranged for a celebrated group of child skaters to appear three times daily. The Gandy Family – Mabel (15), Madde (11) and Alfred (10) - two sisters and their younger brother, had appeared at the Olympia, London, and also at many top continental skating venues. According to this Paris poster they were 'the best paid in the world at 2000 francs per week'. The Hippodrome American Roller Skating Rink, at Place Clichy, Paris, was another European skating venue of Directors Crawford and Wilkins who had set up Ebrington Street.

The Three Gandys - 'The Greatest Juvenile Roller Skaters in the World' *are shown on this postcard. The photo was taken by E. Zwermann and published by Bruno Hunn, both of Hamburg.*

MILLBAY RINKERIES

WEST HOE ROAD, PLYMOUTH.
Resident Manager · · Mr. J. BROCK.

SPECIAL ENGAGEMENT
OF

PROFESSOR

A. A. LENNIE,
COMMENCING

MONDAY, DEC. 13th, 1909
FOR

ONE WEEK ONLY.

SKATERS SHOULD NOT MISS THIS OPPORTUNITY
OF SEEING

The WORLD'S GREATEST GRACEFUL SKATER.

'NUF SED!'

PRICES AS USUAL.
I use the Celebrated RICHARDSON'S' Ball Bearing Skate, exclusively.

Ready for the off! The fancy skater AA Lennie is pictured here on an unused postcard by an anonymous publisher.

AA Lennie, 'the world's greatest graceful skater' was also engaged shortly after, appearing there for a whole week in December 1909. His performance earned him glowing Press coverage:

> *A particularly attractive item this week is supplied by the engagement of Prof. A A Lennie, described as 'the world's greatest fancy and graceful skater' who gives an exhibition at each session. Wonderfully supple, intrepid in difficult twirling tricks and waltzing, the professor is a marvellous performer in truth. Whether it be in sweeping circles and figures on toe or heel, one foot or both, or in graceful swoops from end to end at great pace, like a crimson gull, he proved equally sure and at home and the applause at the close was irresistible.*[6]

The Gandy family and Lennie were just some of the many professional skaters, including Professor Maurice (Morry) Blake, the famous fancy skater, who demonstrated their skills at the Rinkeries over the coming years.

By 1913 Brock had appointed the eminent Professor Jack Weeks, an accomplished exhibition skater who was 'a very demon on skates', as his Floor Manager. A local Press report praised his skating display at a 1913 Carnival:

> *Professor Weeks (who has recently been engaged as an instructor at Millbay) gave one of his wonderful exhibitions of trick skating, having just returned from the Continent, where he has thrilled the skating public for the past twelve months. His tricks are original, he is a fearless skater, and holds a world's championship for spread eagle and loop skating, and no such skating has been yet witnessed in the West of England.[7]*

Another staff member whose skating was much admired was Miss Madge Watson, the lady instructress. Instructors and instructresses would teach basic skating techniques on the learners' or beginners' rink and in 1911 private dance skating lessons were being offered here.

John Brock was to prove himself a most excellent manager, not only ensuring that the population of The Three Towns become proficient in roller skating but always keen to provide the most innovative and amusing entertainment for his clients, whether skaters or spectators.

HIGH JINKS AT THE RINKERIES

Elegant skating events had always been popular in The Three Towns and John Brock of the Millbay Rinkeries lost no time in organising his own. The skating 'Cinderellas' were grand occasions where skaters were obliged to wear evening dress and real photographic postcards were usually on sale

Hawkins appears to have the monopoly on these roller skating postcards. This photograph of a Rinkeries' evening dress carnival is undated.

MILLBAY RINKERIES

WEST HOE ROAD, PLYMOUTH.

Resident Manager - - - *Mr. J. BROCK.*

❋ FIRST GRAND ❋

CINDERELLA

Thursday, Feb. 3rd, 1910.

FOUR SPLENDID PRIZES

One for the Prettiest Lady.
One for the Prettiest Girl.
One for the Most Handsome Gentleman.
One for the Most Handsome Boy.

— VOTING BY POPULAR BALLOT OF THE AUDIENCE. —

EVENING DRESS ONLY will be permitted on the large Rink. Smaller Rink, Skating as usual.

THE GRAND CHALLENGE RACE (Bicycle v. Skates) will be re-run at 9-15 by Messrs. Evans & Briggs.

SPECIAL ENGAGEMENT of the BAND of the

ROYAL GARRISON ARTILLERY

(By kind permission of Col. F. S. Stone., Commanding R.A., S.W.C.D., and Officers)

On this occasion for the Afternoon and Evening Sessions.

PRICES AS USUAL.

Books of 60 tickets may now be had for 30/-

shortly afterwards as souvenirs of the events. The learner's rink continued to operate as usual.

Millbay Rinkeries first 'Grand Cinderella' was held on Thursday 3rd February 1910. Four splendid prizes were offered – for the prettiest lady and girl and for the most handsome gentleman and boy, voting to be by audience ballot. The prizes were certainly generous - a silver cigarette case, a pair of silver military hairbrushes, a silver hair brush and comb in a case and a gold bangle.[8]

This was shortly followed by another 'Cinderella' on Thursday March 3rd, the local newspaper report describing the proceedings as *'probably the most enjoyable skaters have spent at the Millbay*

Rink, Plymouth.' It continued: *'The tasteful scene of decoration carried out under the direction of the Manager(Mr J Brock) caused no little eulogistic comment, and the varied tints in the floral festoons combined with the pretty dresses of the ladies, provided a scene of kaleidoscopic variety.*[9]

Well supported too were the Fancy Dress Carnivals where skaters would devise their own costumes or hire them through national suppliers. Masked Carnivals were also held and a variety of masks could be obtained to add mystery and intrigue to the proceedings. On many occasions Mr Brock supplied masks free to revellers.

The Skating Cinderella of March 3rd 1910. Mr Brock is in the foreground standing next to the young lad and to the right of the elegant lady. Hawkins does the honours again!

Farmyard Carnivals were another attraction, especially at Christmas, when ducks, geese, turkeys and even pigs, were offered as prizes. On one occasion a young lady who won a pig had to transport it home in a taxi! Often special 'Goose Nights' were held with geese given as spot prizes.

Millbay's first Christmas 'farmyard' event took place on Wednesday 22nd December 1909 with livestock to the value of £15 given away. The local *Independent* newspaper gave a detailed account of the celebrations:

The Millbay Rinkeries presented quite a gay appearance on Wednesday last on the occasion of the Xmas

This young lady is all set for a
Confetti Carnival.

A young skater in Gipsy costume on
this photographic postcard taken by R
Stewart, 23 Ship Street, Brighton.

This card was posted to Miss EP Budge, 'Rock
Park', Mount Tavy Road, Tavistock on 5th
September 1910. The message reads: 'How is
this for a Dutchman? No doubt you will be able
to recognise photo, what, what! With love, E'

An enigmatic costume here with
'Answers' written all over it! The card,
which is printed 'A Merry Christmas'
on the reverse was not sent.

114

Farmyard Carnival. Those participating in the races had to be attired to represent something relating to a farmyard. The rink was filled with skaters who hugely enjoyed the fun. The prizes consisted of live poultry, including a turkey, 4 ducks and 4 fowls, and 2 pigs, which were installed in the entrance hall, and added much amusement when brought into the rink – especially when one duck got away from its keeper; it was soon recovered, however.

The report went on to describe the participants, among them being

'numerable dairymaids and milkmaids, wearing print frocks and white aprons, with the print sun bonnets, and carrying stools and milk cans, and very pretty the effect was. In the gentlemen's costumes the most conspicuous was the 'Scarecrow' which was exceptionally good. The 'Sheaf of Corn' was very neat. There was also a 'Cow', 'Poultry Farm', 'Shepherd' … and a large number of ploughmen, farmers and milkmen.'[10]

The hilarious evening included an obstacle race, with egg and spoon and potato races!

The Rinkeries always opened over the Christmas period when Spot Prizes could be won and often valuable prizes such as gold watches were handed out.

The New Year was always seen in with much merrymaking. The festivities at the end of 1909 were especially well supported, as this report describes:

At the Millbay Rinkeries, Plymouth, last evening, the advent of the New Year was appropriately celebrated, skating taking place until midnight, when the doors were thrown open, the various hooters, signals and clock chimes were listened

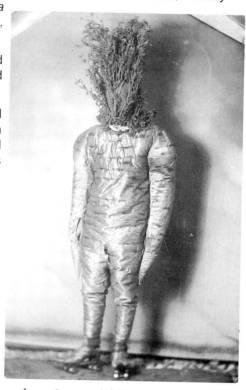

A carrot or parsnip? How does this reveller, all dressed up for a Farmyard Carnival, see his way to skate around?

to, and 'Auld Lang Syne' was sung. The rink was packed all the evening – quite a thousand skaters occupying the floor at one time – and several hundred spectators were present.

Mr Brock also devised '*Red*' nights when skaters had to wear something red and prizes could be won for the best red costume or accessories. There was even a '*Green Night*' on St Patrick's Eve and a '*Grand Midsummer Fancy Dress and White Carnival*' in June. By April 1911 these special colour nights had become so popular that Mr Brock decided to hold a Red Night every Tuesday and a Blue Night each Thursday.

Another diversion for skaters and spectators was '*Have you seen Kelly?*' A mystery man would mingle among both skaters and spectators and the first person to approach him and challenge him would be rewarded.

A Press report of 15th February 1910 describes the search for the elusive 'Kelly':

On Saturday there were 500 skaters on the rink, the great attraction being Kelly who, after being on the floor for a quarter of an hour, was found. Little did anyone dream that a Jack Tar skating round was the much-sought personage. His identification was established

by a Mr E Churchman, a gentleman staying at a local hotel. The reward of £1 was handed to him on the floor by Mr Brock, the popular manager, who is always looking out for something fresh, and next week a well known lady skater will have a special make-up, and the guesser of her name will receive £1. Kelly will be on every Thursday and Saturday. [11]

Other attractions for skater and spectator alike included Graceful Skating Contests, Large Hat and Bow Competition, Maypole Dancing, Confetti Fetes – sometimes billed as 'Confetti Battles', and Coster Carnivals, with prizes for the best Coster costume or hat. A 'China Night' was introduced in November 1913, *'the first of its kind in The Three Towns'*. The report commented on *'such a display of china that one could almost imagine himself in a huge china shop, and each patron was asked to accept a specimen.'* [12]

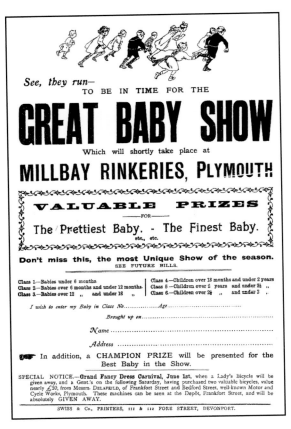

See, they run—
TO BE IN TIME FOR THE

GREAT BABY SHOW

Which will shortly take place at

MILLBAY RINKERIES, PLYMOUTH

VALUABLE PRIZES
——FOR——

The Prettiest Baby. - The Finest Baby.
etc., etc.

Don't miss this, the most Unique Show of the season.
SEE FUTURE BILLS.

Class 1.—Babies under 6 months. | Class 4.—Children over 18 months and under 2 years
Class 2.—Babies over 6 months and under 12 months. | Class 5.—Children over 2 years and under 2½ „
Class 3.—Babies over 12 „ and under 18 „ | Class 6.—Children over 2½ „ and under 3 „

I wish to enter my Baby in Class No...............*Age*.....................................

Brought up on ....

Name ....

Address ....

☞ In addition, a CHAMPION PRIZE will be presented for the
Best Baby in the Show.

SPECIAL NOTICE.—**Grand Fancy Dress Carnival, June 1st,** when a Lady's Bicycle will be
given away, and a Gent.'s on the following Saturday, having purchased two valuable bicycles, value
nearly £20, from Messrs. DELAFIELD, of Frankfort Street and Bedford Street, well-known Motor and
Cycle Works, Plymouth. These machines can be seen at the Depôt, Frankfort Street, and will be
absolutely GIVEN AWAY.

SWISS & Co., PRINTERS, 111 & 112 FORE STREET, DEVONPORT.

Another of Brock's ideas was a Baby Competition where, at the very first event of this kind at the Rinkeries on Saturday 18th June 1910, a surprising 200 babies were entered with over 2000 visiting the event. With so many entries received the result was not announced until 10.30pm![13] Another 'Great Baby Show' took place on Wednesday 25th July 1917.

Often a packed Millbay Rinkeries programme included sports events – either of the fun kind, or serious sporting contests – and these proved to be just as popular as the graceful skating sessions and galas.

Chapter Ten

Roller Skating Sports

Almost from the outset numerous sporting activities and sporting events were introduced to the Rinkeries programme. Many were of the lighthearted kind such as musical chairs – for which there were separate circles of chairs for ladies and gentlemen - and all kinds of races: Ambulance Race (for three gents!), Egg and Spoon, Backward, Balloon, Butter Keg Race (ladies), Hoop Race (ladies), Novelty Race (gents), Obstacle Race (gents), Potato Race (gents), Relay Race (2 ladies, 2 gents), Sack Race (with ankles tied), Three legged Race (gents), Wheelbarrow and Candle races – all on skates of course. Many of these innovative races appeared nightly during a 'Great Rinkhana Week' in February 1912.

The candle race had ladies taking part and they found it very difficult keeping their candles alight while skating at a brisk pace. The obstacle race on 22nd December, 1909, *'caused a great deal of merriment, as the competitors had to first jump a plank, then crawl through a barrel, jump another plank, and finally run up a plank and jump off.'*[1]

Skittles competitions were another attraction. Sixteen skittles were placed on the rink and skaters had to negotiate around them without knocking any down, rather like a slalom event. A prize of one guinea was offered to anyone, lady or gentleman, who could perform this feat.

A publicity flier for the Rinkeries, dated 25th September 1912, announced: *'Look out for the American Bowling Alley – Nothing like it this side of London!'* - certainly a first for Plymouth and a forerunner to the current Mega Bowl at the Barbican Leisure Park.

The 'Steeplechase' was another popular but frivolous event where ladies and gentlemen were decked out in 'equine contraptions' - hobby horse type outfits - and had to surmount obstacles on skates, a far from easy task.

On Wednesday 11th September 1917 eight horses entered for the 'Millbay Steeplechase'. It was reported that *'these were ridden chiefly by soldiers and sailors, who at an alarming rate dashed over the hurdles and took imaginary water jumps, which caused uproarious amusement.*[2]

The impression often given was that the 'horses' were, in fact, real ones as a 'flyer' for Wednesday 8th March 1916 informed the public that *'the horses have now recovered from the influenza and the race will now take place'*.

*Rinkeries manager, John Brock, proudly shows off
four gallant chargers for an equestrian skating event*

*Brock restrains the mounts of
these two elegant lady 'riders'*

*Members of the Millbay hockey team are ready to push the
'roller speedboats' in this photo taken in November 1935.*

Again, always keen to take advantage of any publicity, Mr Brock stated through the Press that on 31st March 1910 a Polo Match would take place and that horses were already in training at Crownhill for this event![3]

Punting Races were another diversion, the wheeled punts controlled by the pushers and the seated occupants on skates. Sometimes these were billed as either a 'Boat Race', the one promoted by the Millbay Rink Hockey Club on 30th April 1913 causing *'endless fun and several 'capsized' amid much laughter',*[4] or as 'Roller Speedboats' as advertised in November 1935 and seen in this photograph. On Thursday 23rd November 1911 a 'Roman Chariot Race' was included in the programme.

Almost every kind of sport imaginable was added to Brock's entertainment, a 'unique Archery competition on skates' being part of the programme – starting every afternoon from Saturday, 31st December 1910.

Tug of War contests were held between the Army and Navy, always on roller skates, one taking place on January 6th 1910. At one event there was even a tug of war against live donkeys! That same evening there was a skating race between 14 service personnel who had never donned skates before and another race in which skaters were pitted against cyclists.[5]

More serious skate races were arranged between speed skaters. On 1st Dec 1909 the Rinkeries' first Amateur Two Mile Race was supported by a record attendance. A newspaper report gave full details:

> The starter was Mr J Brock and Mr RF Davis, NCU, was timekeeper. Mr WM Duggua, as judge, had a responsible task. Sixteen started in the race, and C Briggs, wearing Polytechnic CC colours, got clear away, with F Ballisat next. They strung out at once, but in the third lap Brigg's skate came off, when he had fifteen yards lead, with Lapthorne going well. There was a surprise in store, however, and the result was: 1. S Jane; 2. F Ballisat; 3. G Lapthorne, all members of the newly-formed Plymouth Skating Club. The time was 16 mins. 16 secs. The three prizes were of a very handsome nature. Next Wednesday a professional race takes place.[6]

As well as being challenged by cyclists, experts in fast skating were often matched against local sprint champions on foot. On St Patrick's Night, Thursday 17th March 1910, RD Duff, Amateur Champion of The Three Towns, ran against F Ballisat on skates, the latter conceding 45 seconds start.

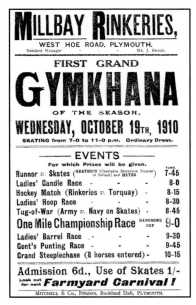

These types of sporting events often featured in a mixed programme, and where several contests occurred the evening entertainment was often billed as a 'Gymkhana'. The local Press report of a Gymkhana held on 19th October 1910 gives the full flavour of the sporting evening and also mentions some local personalities.

The first Gymkhana of the season was held at the Millbay Rinkeries last evening. The sports sheet was an extremely interesting one, and was enjoyed to the utmost by the large audience. For the efficient manner in which the programme was carried out, Mr Brock, with his staff, deserves unstinted commendation.

The Gymkhana started with one of the tit-bits of the evening – a contest between Tom Heathcock, Saltash (the well known champion marathon runner) and G Hayes (the erstwhile skating champion). The skater conceded two laps in nine, and was well beaten by Heathcock, the margin separating them at the finish being about 110 yards – 7/8ths of a lap.

The ladies Candle Race was cleverly won by Miss Radley. The Tug of War between the Army and Navy was stubbornly fought and resulted in a win for the Army (Royal Marines).

The great race of the evening was, of course, the One Mile Championship Race, for which a handsome cup was offered by the management. It was won after a hard tussle by Mr WJ Julian.

The Hockey Match between the Rinkeries who, by the way, are an unbeaten team, and Torquay was strenuously contested. At the interval no score had been registered, but in the second moiety Evans, Lillicrap and Bowden each notched a point for Millbay, the homesters thus winning by three goals to nil.

The gents' Punting Race was skillfully won by Mr F Eva. The Steeplechase, for which eight horses had entered, caused uncontrolled merriment, and after many tumbles Mr Bawden cantered over the line an easy winner.[7]

ROLLER HOCKEY AND FOOTBALL

Skate hockey was a very popular, well supported sport and one which was taken seriously in Plymouth and other West Country towns. The first roller hockey matches date from 1870 and were originally called 'Roller Polo'.

Typical roller hockey boots.
These are HAMACO No.31 'Tenacity'

The Plymouth Promenade Pier Skating Rink had been one of the first local rinks to inaugurate a club to promote both hockey and football. The Manager, J Higson, had called a meeting for the 29th November 1909 at which the Plymouth Skating Club was formed. It was to be affiliated to the National Skating Association and its rules would be those of the original Plymouth S.C.

The following officers were appointed: President J Higson; Vice-President Mr Duggua [a skate maker of King Street]; Hon. Secretary Mr B J Lloyd; Captain Mr F Cowles; Vice-Captain Mr Dicks; Treasurer Mr S Jane; Committee: C Briggs; S Lethbridge; AC Bidgeway; P Sweet; G Lapthorne; Messrs. Medland and Pooley. The annual subscription was fixed at 2s 6d per annum for gentlemen and 1s 6d for ladies.[8]

The Ebrington Street Rink and Millbay Rinkeries each had a roller hockey team. The Rinkeries' Hockey Club was launched in March 1910 and Gentlemen and Ladies teams were drawn up. A picture and report of the newly-formed men's team featured in the national skating magazine *World on Wheels* in October 1910. A much later photograph shows the Millbay Rinkeries hockey team in the early 1930s.

The Rinkeries team had many hockey successes and regularly competed against local teams and those from other Westcountry rinks such as Truro, Torquay and Newton Abbott. They even played host to a team from the famous London Olympia and on another occasion welcomed the Welsh roller hockey champions, Merthyr. Millbay won this game 4-0.[9]

A team picture of St Austell Rink Hockey Club players taken c.1910. This was just one of the many South West sides which competed against the Millbay Club. The postcard bears no publisher details but a pencilled note on the reverse gives the Hon. Secretary as H Thomas, Greenaway Villa, St Austell.

PLYMOUTH.—The Millbay (Plymouth) Rink Hockey Club only came into existence six months ago, and no hockey being played in the three summer months their active operations so far have been very limited. The team, however, in that short space did well and hold an unbeaten certificate, their record up to date being—Played 7, Won 6, Drawn 1, Lost 0. This club is very anxious to foster hockey in the West and are endeavouring to form a Hockey League for Devon and Cornwall. The secretary desires it to be known that if any club should be touring the West he would like to hear from them with the view of making a fixture. Notice as early as possible should be given to H. Orgel, 9, Athenæum-street, Plymouth.

THE MILLBAY RINK HOCKEY CLUB, PLYMOUTH.
Standing: A. E. Budd, C. McDonald, J. Brock, Esq. (Manager), F. C. Collins, A. B. Batchelor.
Seated: F. Vanstone, A. E. Evans (Vice-Captain), F. R. Lillicrap (Capt.), B. Bowden, H. Orgel (Hon. Sec.)

MILLBAY RINKERIES,
WEST HOE ROAD, PLYMOUTH.
Resident Manager — Mr. J. Banex.

WEDNESDAY, OCTOBER 26TH, 1910

GRAND RETURN

HOCKEY MATCH

MILLBAY
(Undefeated Champions of the West)
VERSUS

EBRINGTON STREET

AT 9 P.M. PROMPT.

Will Ebrington Street reverse the Last Result?

Owing to the Jockeys having run the Wrong Course on Wednesday Last the

GRAND STEEPLECHASE
Will be RE-RUN, at 9-30 p.m.

Time and Prices as Usual.

Mitchell & Co., Printers, Buckland Hall, Plymouth.

The Rinkeries' first roller hockey team, featured in the national magazine World on Wheels, *October 1910.*

The Rinkeries hockey team line-up, mid 1930s

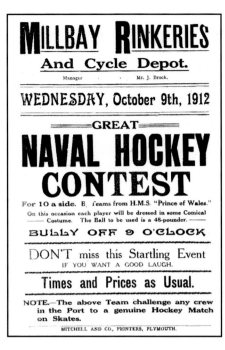

Often games were held against local and Services teams with the visitors either on foot or on skates. In October 1912 the Millbay Champions, as they were known, challenged a combined team from HMS Carnarvon and R.M.L.I., the Champions fielding five men to their opponents ten.

Hockey matches, however, were not always taken seriously. This poster advertising a 'Great Naval Hockey Contest' had each player dressed in a comical costume and the ball used was a '48-pounder'!

Football matches on skates were sometimes held but they were not as popular as skate hockey. A Rinkeries Football Club was formed in May 1910, the first match being a seven-a-side game against a Devonport team. The ball was kicked off by Ivy Brock, the manager's daughter, and the result was a 1-0 win for the home team. Matches were to be arranged every Wednesday.[10]

Having such a large expanse of maple flooring it was not long before John Brock decided to utilise the space for other sporting events. On Wednesday 30th October 1912 the Rinkeries was made available to the South Devon and Cornwall Harriers for a 'Grand 2-Mile Walking Championship'.

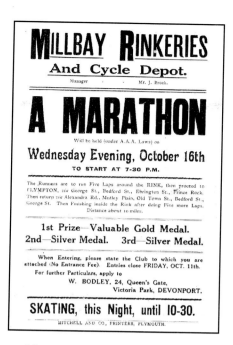

MILLBAY RINKERIES

And Cycle Depot.

Manager - - Mr. J. Brock.

A MARATHON

Will be held (under A.A.A. Laws) on

Wednesday Evening, October 16th

TO START AT 7-30 P.M.

The Runners are to run Five Laps around the RINK, then proceed to
PLYMPTON, via George St., Bedford St., Ebrington St., Prince Rock.
Then return via Alexandra Rd., Mutley Plain, Old Town St., Bedford St.,
George St. Then Finishing inside the Rink after doing Five more Laps.
Distance about 10 miles.

1st Prize—Valuable Gold Medal.
2nd—Silver Medal. 3rd—Silver Medal.

When Entering, please state the Club to which you are
attached (No Entrance Fee). Entries close FRIDAY, OCT. 11th.
For further Particulars, apply to
W. BODLEY, 24, Queen's Gate,
Victoria Park, DEVONPORT.

SKATING, this Night, until 10-30.

MITCHELL AND CO., PRINTERS, PLYMOUTH.

MARATHONS AND BADMINTON

By October 1912 the rink was curiously billed as 'Millbay Rinkeries and Cycle Depot' (although this title seldom appeared on later posters) and on the 16th of that month it sponsored a Marathon to be held under AAA laws with gold and silver medals awarded. There was no entrance fee and details could be obtained from W Bodley, 24 Queen's Gate, Victoria Park, Devonport. The programme sets out the following route:

> 'The Runners are to run Five Laps around the RINK, then proceed to PLYMPTON, via George Street, Bedford Street, Ebrington Street, Prince Rock. Then return via Alexandra Road, Mutley Plain, Old Town Street, Bedford Street, George Street. Then finishing inside the Rink after doing Five more Laps. Distance about 10 miles.'

Brock also welcomed the *Hoe and Devonport Badminton Club* to use the arena every Monday and Thursday from the 31st March to 14th November. The *HDBC* leaflet for 1910-11, contained in Brock's *Cuttings Book*, informs its members they could skate at much reduced rates. In 1912-13 the United Services Badminton Club were meeting in the Rinkeries every Friday afternoon from 22nd November until the following April. The courts were private and away from the main rink.

Proposed Rinkeries Swimming Bath

By the end of 1912 Brock, now the owner of the Rinkeries, had other ideas for the learners' rink and intended using it for different purposes. An interesting series of newspaper cuttings giving details of his extraordinary plan can be found in his *Cuttings Book*. They outline his proposal for a much-needed swimming bath for The Three Towns. One of the first Press reports on this topic appeared in September 1911. Entitled *'Plymouth Swimming Bath: New Scheme to Meet Public Needs'* it gave comprehensive details of Brock's vision:

> *A scheme for the establishment of an indoor public swimming bath for Plymouth is in course of formation. Plymouth is sadly behind many other seaside towns in this matter, and it is no credit to the municipality that the needs of the public may have to be met from a private, or semi-private source. The scheme originates with Mr John Brock, of the Millbay Rinkeries. Negotiations, at present in a preliminary stage, are of a somewhat intricate and complicated character, but full details will be submitted very shortly. The public will have the opportunity of becoming directly and actively interested in the new venture.*

> *The proposal is to transform one portion of the Millbay rinkeries, known as the "learners' rink" into a swimming bath …The transformation would necessitate the removal of the present floor and the erection of galleries, dressing boxes, &c. At one end of the bath would be a springboard, chute, &c.*

> *Interviewed last night, Mr Brock said the scheme would commend itself to the public, inasmuch as the conditions under which the public could participate in the scheme would be easy, and the prospects of success great. He had already secured promises of support from clubs interested in water polo and such like games, and had not the least doubt the provision of a swimming bath of the kind indicated would be eagerly welcomed by all classes. A company would shortly be formed to acquire the whole of the Rinkeries and provide the bath, which would be open in connection with the large rink.*

> *'The popularity of the rink', said Mr Brock, 'may be gauged from the fact that during the three years it has been opened it has been visited by over a million persons.'*

> *Replying to questions Mr Brock said it would be a salt water bath. There would be separate days for ladies and for gentlemen. He*

believed the necessary alterations could be affected within two months. Plans had already been prepared, and would be on view in the course of a day or two after the completion of present negotiations.[11]

A series of meetings were held to discuss the project. The second meeting, attended by local swimming clubs, was held at the Millbay rink presided over by Mr FW Skardon, ably assisted by FA Wiblin, the architect, and EG Pope. The clubs were all in favour of the new scheme as this press item explains:

The local swimming associations were well represented, and after a short discussion it was proposed by Mr W Sweet, Treasurer of the Port of Plymouth Swimming Association, seconded by Mr Kellaway, Secretary of the Plymouth Amateur Swimming Society, and agreed that the two local swimming clubs should be called together at an early date next week with a view to having particulars of the scheme laid before them.

Mr GH Lavers expressed himself perfectly satisfied with the suitability of the site and the practicability of the proposal, and also as to the source from which the salt water would be drawn. He had every confidence that with a proper measure of support the baths would prove a success. That view was endorsed by several prominent swimmers present.

The article continues with an outline of plans for the baths:

The plans, as designed by Mr Wiblin, provide for a swimming bath 100 feet long by about 30 feet wide, so as to meet the requirements of League matches and there will be about sixty dressing boxes. At one end the bath will be 3ft. 6ins.in depth and at the other 7ft. The salt water will be drawn from outside the Great Western Docks, and a gallery will be built around the bath for spectators. It is proposed to form a limited liability company, with a capital of £4,000, divided into £1 shares, to meet the cost of the combined scheme of bath and rinkeries.

As was to be expected, there were the usual letters to the Press, this one signed 'Natator' was dated the 28th September 1911.

PROPOSED THREE TOWNS SWIMMING BATH: Sir – I note with interest the account of last night's public meeting with respect to the above. I am fully in sympathy with the movement to provide a local swimming bath which would undoubtedly supply a much-needed requirement, would greatly foster the useful art of natation, especially amongst the young, and prove a decided attraction to the district.

During the past few years many of the most prominent and influential men of The Three Towns have publicly advocated the provision of swimming baths. I would therefore ask those 'in the swim' to answer, through your columns, the two following questions:

a)   Have any well-known gentlemen been interviewed upon this matter? If so, with what results?

b)   What are the names of the promoters of this present scheme?

Prompt answers to these questions would supply information not now before the public, and should do much to ensure the success of what I believe to be a much-needed and well-conceived scheme for the provision of a swimming bath.

Discussions on the proposed swimming baths carried on well into October 1911 and criticism of the local Council were strangely reminiscent of similar comments made much later in 2006-7 concerning the provision of swimming bath facilities in Plymouth!

Another meeting of interested parties was held at the Western Law Courts on Thursday 12th October, presided over by Mr JS Argall. Mr FW Skardon gave some financial details, estimating that from the Rinkeries a year's return would be £2,506 with the swimming bath bringing in £845. The working expenses would be £2,066, leaving a profit of £1,285.

The meeting went on to criticise the Council:

The Chairman pointed out that in six years they had had six Mayors who had advocated a swimming bath. They ought to show some interest in the proposal. Mr Skardon said he had approached these gentlemen and they were a little reluctant to respond. If the Corporation proposal with regard to Beaumont House were dropped, perhaps they would look upon the scheme more favourably.

In the course of discussion it was explained that the scheme would entail the purchase of the nineteen-year Rinkeries' lease together with the considerable equipment and rolling stock. A figure of £1,000 had been set aside for that and the construction of the new bath would cost £2,100. Asked who the promoters would be, Mr Skardon said that Mr Brock had the right to purchase for a certain period and then he could sell off the lease to anybody.

The length of the lease appeared to be a stumbling block and the meeting was adjourned so that Mr Skardon could make further legal enquiries regarding the cost of the freehold.

Nothing came of the 1911 talks but the subject of an indoor swimming bath for Plymouth became a topic for further discussion in 1925 and resurfaced again much later in 1932. The proposal for a 'baths scheme' was put before council and it was agreed that *'swimming baths were a necessity for the full education and for the benefit of the health of the children of the city and that they should support the minute.'* However, when the subject was brought before Council on the 16th January 1932 the fact that it was proposed to raise revenue by issuing council bonds so there would be no call on the rates did not meet with approval. The motion was quickly defeated with no discussion at all, except for brief speeches from the mover, Mr CH Townsend, and his seconder.[12]

An 'Interested Townsman', again advocated the Rinkeries as an ideal site for a swimming bath, and wrote to the *Western Evening Herald:*

Sir, Why any discussion on the proposed indoor swimming bath at Plymouth when we have such fine facilities as the "Rinkeries" at Millbay Road, which were suggested as far back as 1925?. Here is a building all ready for conversion at a small cost; near the sea, rail and centre of the city. Surely such a site could be procured at a reasonable figure and made into a paying proposition? Our councillors, when discussing such a proposal, do not seem to know that such buildings are at hand waiting for development. Such a scheme is long overdue in Plymouth and would justify itself in a very short period and eventually become one of the city's amenities.[13]

The Rinkeries swimming bath never materialised. On the 12th May 1928 the Ballard Institute, a club for boys, was opened, financed by the philanthropist Albert Casanova Ballard. He had purchased the old Millbay Soap Works above the Rinkeries, had demolished them, and erected his new Institute on the site. Fortunately for Mr Brock his part of the building had been left untouched. This first Ballard building did have a swimming bath but only for the boy members.

The public pool in the new Ballard Institute in Crescent Avenue, Millbay Road, which opened in June 1963 to replace the original one, will be better remembered by Plymouth residents today.

The original Ballard Institute which opened in 1928. The Rinkeries entrance is just visible on the far left. This fine photographic postcard has no publisher or date

WRESTLING AND BOXING AT THE RINKERIES

It appears that during the years after Brock had become the owner and proprietor of the Rinkeries he had from time to time leased out the premises to various persons. Many of the lessees used the premises for boxing and wrestling and promoters included Jack Bodinetz, L & P Promotions, Star Promotions and the Exeter promoter Harry Williams.

For a short time up to 1933 the Rinkeries had been leased to the Smith Brothers who also promoted bouts at the Millbay site. After their relinquishment of the lease Brock again opened the Rinkeries for the winter skating session as usual. He was also promoting wrestling and boxing himself, often in conjunction with Jack Merrett, the former manager of the Pier Pavilion. Boxing was very popular with locals and servicemen and the Rinkeries was billed as *'The Wembley of the West'*.

Details can be found of a 1936 one year lease on the Rinkeries, West Hoe Road, between John Brock and Frederick Hubert Barnard, sports promoter, at £25 per annum.[14]

One of the last promoters of a Rinkeries boxing evening was Plymothian AE 'Archie' Cload of the BBBC – British Boxing Board of Control – who

MILLBAY SKATING RINK
PLYMOUTH.

FRIDAY, DECEMBER 22nd.
Doors open 7.15. Commence 8 p.m.

L. & P. PROMOTIONS present a
SENSATIONAL INTERNATIONAL PROGRAMME OF
ALL-IN WRESTLING
THE KING OF SPORTS.

Stupendous International Heavyweight Contest
(100 minutes, 2 falls or K.O.)

ATHOLL OAKELEY

(Britain). Weight 14st. Heavyweight Champion of Great
Britain 1930-31-32-33. Educated Clifton College and
Sandhurst. The greatest Athlete produced by Britain
since the war. Has met and defeated most of the
principal Continental Champions since his return from
his wonderfully successful tour of U.S.A. and Canada
1931. VERSUS

MARCEL DOUVINET

(France). Weight 16st. Heavyweight Champion of
Paris. One of the greatest Continental wrestlers. Noted
for his great strength.

Very Special International Contest
60 mins. 2 falls.

BULLDOG BILL CARNON

(Fishguard). 16st 8lbs. Heavyweight Champion of
Wales and leading contender for the British Championship. Recently returned from 3 years tour of U.S.A
where he met and defeated many of the best. V

LEN FRANKLIN

Elstree. 14st. Southern Champion of Britain. Winner of
1932 Eliminating Tournament for British Title
Wrestling's gift to sculptors.

Super International Heavyweights 60 mins. 2 falls.

TONY BAER v. VAN DUTZ

13st. (Glasgow). Scotland's | 18st. (Holland). Noted
tabloid Heavyweight who | through this country and
recently beat David Arm- | abroad for his rough and
strong and Rudi Barbu the | u n o r t h o d o x methods.
Roumanian Champion. | Watch him try them on
 | Tony !

Lightheavyweight Contest.
RICHARD WILLS v. PAT O'NEIL
Newbiggin. Lightheavy- | Belfast. A future champion
weight Champion of | of Ireland.
Britain.

REFEREE SPIDER HARVEY.

POPULAR PRICES :
Ringside Reserved | Stalls Reserved | Unreserved
5/- | 3/6 | 2/6 1/3
 | (including Tax) |

DON'T MISS THIS GREAT CHRISTMAS SENSATION.
Book Early at Mount Pleasant Hotel, Millbay Road.
'Phone 1007

BRUNEL HOTEL
CLOSE TO THE RINKERIES

FULLY LICENSED

YOUR RENDEZVOUS DURING INTERVAL
Sportsmen always Welcome

PLYMOUTH
Manager DICK BURT

* SPORTING *

MOIR STREET
PLYMOUTH
CLUB

Ten Three-Minute Rounds Middle-weight Contest

BATTLING CHARLIE | FREDDIE

PARKIN MILLS
versus

MANSFIELD—NORTHERN AREA MIDDLEWEIGHT CHAMPION whose
brilliant win over Nat Franks surprised Plymothians. Has defeated Tommy Martin,
Jack Hyams, and also drawn and lost on points to Ginger Sadd.

BOURNEMOUTH—A COMING CHAMPION. Last narrow points verdict against
Ginger Sadd, recently. Defeated Dave McClave, Eddie McQuire (South Africa),
Moe Moss (London), Yorkey Bentley (Canada), Harry Lister (New Zealand), Paul
Schaeffer, Red Pullen and many others.

on Friday 21st July 1939 brought Freddie Mills to the Rinkeries. The programme billed him as 'a coming champion'. They were to be proved right!

The very last programme to be found is for a boxing event dated Monday 14th August 1939, just three weeks before war was declared. However, it is clear from a 1939 undated newspaper report found in Brock's *Cuttings Book*, which most likely appeared at the onset of World War Two, that he did intend to promote more boxing events as well as offering the Rinkeries venue as a training centre for the sport. The article, headed *'PLYMOUTH REVIVAL: Service Authorities To Be Approached'* reads:

> *Movement for the resumption of boxing in Plymouth is being pursued. Mr John Brock, proprietor of Millbay Rinkeries, has expressed his willingness to co-operate in any movement for the benefit of servicemen by granting all the facilities the hall can offer.*

> *Mr Harry Reynolds, ex-featherweight champion of the Western Area, states he is prepared to act as boxing instructor to the novices. Reynolds was featherweight champion when, as a 15-years-old boy he was serving in the Royal Navy. Mr Dick Burt, an old area champion, is also anxious to be of service.*

> *There is a proposal for commanding officers to be approached for their views on the matter, and to have submitted to them details of boxing tournaments during the last war when wounded convalescents were admitted free.*

Unfortunately, the Blitz was soon to put an end to any further sports or skating events at the Rinkeries.

CHAPTER ELEVEN

MILITARY MATTERS

It was inevitable in a strong military area such as The Three Towns that servicemen would join the skaters and be made very welcome at both the Ebrington Street and Millbay rinks. The local Press recorded many soldiers and sailors winning prizes and service teams were regularly invited to participate in various sporting events. So successful were John Brock's efforts to ensure that there was a strong military presence at his rink that in 1917 Brock was advertising the Rinkeries as *'Home of Amusement for the Navy and Army'*.

Many military bands featured in the special Sunday concerts held at the Rinkeries as skating was not allowed on the Sabbath. The Royal Garrison Artillery Band – who sometimes played at skating dances and Cinderellas - often appeared as did the band of HM Royal Marines, the 2nd Battalion Royal Scots, 4th Battalion Middlesex Regt. and the 1st Battalion the Gordon Highlanders. During the 1910 winter season the Rinkeries band which accompanied the skating was led by Mr Miller, bandmaster of the Territorials, Devonport.[1]

The Rinkeries was very popular with serving officers and in October 1910 the following announcement appeared in the local Press:

A club is being formed by the officers of the United Services. The first evening was held on Tuesday 5.15 to 7pm., when a goodly attendance of officers were in evidence (with their friends). Great credit is due to Lieut. Money R.N. for the enthusiasm he has shown in organising the club, he being the originator. Any officer desirous of joining the club can apply for full particulars to Lieut. Money R.N., Millbay Rinkeries, Plymouth.[2]

A month later membership of the USPRC - *United Services Private Rink Club* - had reached 150 and members, with their friends, often made up a party of over 300.[3] The Tuesday meetings were so popular that the early evening weekly sessions were also offered on Fridays from December 1910, as this announcement shows.

𝔐illbay 𝔑inkeries.

DEAR SIR OR MADAM,

As many members of the U.S.P.R.C. have expressed a desire to have two club days a week, I have been in consultation with Lieut. Money, R.N., and the following is thought a good idea :—

The Rink Club to have the floor on Fridays at the same time as on Tuesdays—5 to 7 p.m.

The following prices will be charged for admission—

Holders of Skating Tickets—6d. with own Skates,
1/- without.
Holders of Non-Skating Tickets—3d., or with use of Skates, 1/-
Guests, introduced by a member, Skating—1/-,
Non-Skating—3d.

The Rinkeries will provide the Band and will take all moneys.

It is to be understood that this is done to provide a second day per week for the **Members of the Club, and that only Members of the Club and their guests will be admitted.**

It is thought that this scheme would be better than increasing the subscription for each member who wished to make use of the second day.

The 2nd day will start on Friday, 2nd December.

J. BROCK, MANAGER.

Per LIEUT. N. A. K. MONEY, R.N.

Any event with a military theme always proved an attraction at the Rinkeries. In July 1913 it was announced that a 'Summer Carnival' in August would included a mock war, imitating Naval manoeuvres. A dozen 'warships', manned by Blue Jackets and fully armed, would make an attack on a fort and everything was being arranged to represent a 'mimic war'.[4]

Brock did much to boost the morale of troops stationed in The Three Towns, inviting them to join in the Rinkeries fun and so take their minds off the loneliness of service life. Brock's *Cuttings Book* contains an interesting telegraph dated 11th March 1913 from General Penton, Devonport, confirming that *'Territorial Force is included in Army under King's Regulations.'* Brock was obviously anxious to afford the TA the same privileges he gave regular soldiers.

During World War One Brock did all he could for service personnel and new recruits. His *Cuttings Book* contains other telegrams and memos from several regiments' commanding officers thanking Brock for his kind invitations to their men. A telegram dated 9th April 1917 from V Maslov, Commander, Russian Navy, is reproduced here.

~~H.I.R.M.S.~~ "ASKOLD."   No.

                        at   Devonport

                                            Dockyard.

                                            April   9th *1917*

Mr. Brock,
    West Hoe Road,
        Plymouth

Dear Sir,

        The crew of "Askold" desire to express their thanks
for a most enjoyable evening at your Rink, and wish you every
success for the future.

                            Yours Truly,   *V. Maslov*

                    Commander Russian Navy

HIRMS Askold

RD Miller, the Adjutant, writing on behalf of the Major Commanding, South African Heavy Artillery, sent this memo dated 17th October 1917:

I have to thank you for your invitation for 50 men of this unit to your rink on Saturday. The men are being informed that they will be made welcome.

The Evening Herald of 24th October reported that:

'At Millbay Rink yesterday, by permission of the Major-in-Command, fifty men of the South African Heavy Artillery were entertained. After skating and a tea three hearty cheers were given to Mr Brock. One of the men said this was the first time they had been entertained, and they should always remember it.'

Another memo sent from Crownhill Barracks on 3rd November 1917 and signed by the Captain Adjutant, 38th Battalion. Royal Fusiliers, is reproduced here.

```
        J.Brock. Esq.,
          Millbay Rinkeries,
            Plymouth.
            . . . . . . . . . . .


        Dear Sir,

                    I much regret that owing to illness I have not
            sooner acknowledged your kind invitation for 50 men of this
            Battalion to visit your rink to-day.
                        I need hardly say the invitation is much appreciated.
                        Yours Faithfully.


The much will assi a law                              Captain and Adjutant
           J /m.                                  38th Bn.Royal Fusiliers.
        Crownhill Bks.
          Plymouth.
          3. 11. 17
```

In September 1914 Brock wrote identical letters to both the *Western Daily Mercury* and the *Western Morning News* expressing his view that more should be done to entertain the troops:

> *Sir, - I notice that several kind ladies and gentlemen are doing all they can to make our soldiers spend a pleasant evening in the Guildhall, but the soldier wants something more than that. If they would only follow Miss S Carey's example, I am sure every soldier would be thankful. There are scores of shops in the town, besides private houses, which have surplus bread, meat, fish, etc. If this could be collected, and give each soldier or sailor a good, free supper, there would not be half the drunkenness you now see about the streets. What is bread and jam to stay a man from 5pm until about 7 next day? I shall be only too pleased to help anyone interested.*

Brock played his own part in helping the troops and the Rinkeries also became a collection centre for book donations for servicemen:

> *Five hundred soldiers took over Millbay Rinkeries last evening. By permission of the officers, the men were allowed to skate from 6.30 to 8, and nearly 200 availed themselves of the opportunity. There were also Stentorphone selections. Miss Brock sent books for the men, and for these there was a great demand. Books sent to the rink will be distributed by Mr Brock.* [5]

Entertainments were put on, one concert party organised and presented by the Misses Knight included the Misses Webber, Finch and Horne. Messrs. French and White, Private Eddolls, Sergeant Billett, Lieutenant Benon and Private Johnston also took part. The Concert Secretary was Lieutenant Cripps.[6] Another entertaining evening, under the patronage of Captain Speke and officers, had included a Mr F Bickford with his marionettes and conjuring.

The 5th Devon recruits were also lavishly entertained:

From funds subscribed by friends and tradesmen, under the control of a committee comprising Mrs Gurney, the Misses Austen (3), Miss Young, Mrs Bickford, Mrs Evans, Miss Bash, and Mr J Brock, 109 Recruits of the 5th Devon Regiment (Territorials) stationed at Plymouth Drill Hall, were last night entertained to supper at Millbay Rinkeries, which had been placed at the disposal of the committee by Mr Brock. The tables were tastefully decorated, and the men, who were accompanied by their officer, Captain EM Leest, were provided with ham sandwiches, cake, hot chip potatoes, and tea, the members of the committee presiding at the tables. Afterwards Miss B Austen handed each man a packet of cigarettes and a box of matches, and then, at the invitation of Mr Brock, the men indulged in skating.

Miss Austen is Honorary Secretary of the committee, with Miss F Austen Hon. Treasurer, and with the permission of Captain Leest, the men will be again be provided with supper this evening and each Monday and Thursday as long as the funds permit. The recruits greatly appreciated the entertainment, and after singing 'It's a Long Way to Tipperary' gave cheers for the committee and all those who had contributed to their enjoyment.[7]

Sadly the Rinkeries' hospitality temporarily ended when the recruits were posted elsewhere but not before a 'thank you' letter had been sent through the local Press:

ENTERTAINMENTS TO MILLBAY RECRUITS: Sir – You kindly inserted notices of entertainment given at the Millbay Rinkeries to the recruits quartered in the Drill Hall. Will you allow me through your columns to tell our kind supporters that for the present these suppers will be discontinued? Recruits will be passed so quickly from the Drill Hall to other places that they will not need entertainment. We have met with a generous response to our appeal for help, and gifts in kind have been received from a large number of ladies and gentlemen. Gifts of money have also been received, which have been duly accounted for and audited, and we have in hand nearly £8, which we propose to hold over till need for again helping the recruits occurs. I take this opportunity of warmly thanking all who have helped us, especially Mr Brock for the loan of the Rinkeries and for electric light, and Mrs Evans, who kindly catered for us. We are sure that we can rely on their continued support when required.

DF GURNEY, 1a Leigham Street, Plymouth.[8]

Many of the Rinkeries clientele were recruited in World War One as well as some of Brock's staff. On May 10th 1916 a presentation took place following a hockey match between the home team and 'the pick of the Navy and Army'.

Mr Brock presented the captain of the Millbay team (Mr W Dean) with a wristlet watch on behalf of the members and himself. Mr Brock said that although he was sorry to lose Mr Dean, he was sure that he was doing his duty by deciding to serve his country, and trusted that all skaters would follow his example. Mr Dean thanked Mr Brock, and said the watch would always remind him of the good old Millbay Rink.[9]

A selection of local advertisements for skates and skating contained in the 1910 booklet 'Rinking: How – Why – When' dated 1910

Chapter Twelve

A Portrait of John Brock

The Rinkeries manager, John Brock, with four young skaters, all wearing 'rollers'.
The young girl on the right has a most amazing hair style!
The photo was taken in 1910 by Haddons, 8 Union Street.

John Brock was a very colourful, outgoing character, a superb manager and organiser who always seemed to have 'a happy knack of continually introducing new and novel features which keep up the interest without any signs of flagging'.[1] In Press reports he was described as an energetic manager, 'having great powers of organisation'. He was also a proficient figure and fancy skater.

The Brocks were a very well-known Plymouth family. John, born 'Jacob Nathan' to Lewis and Henrietta Brock on 28th May 1867 at 67 Cecil Street, was the fourth of their five sons. This extract from the *Susser Archive*, a thesis by Rabbi Bernard Susser, gives an excellent potted history of the Plymouth Brocks:

> *Between the two World Wars some of the more assimilated [Jewish] families began to take up a wider range of business activity. The Brock family, for example, was old-established in Plymouth. Eleazar (George) Brook (as the name first appeared) was a tailor in Plymouth when his son, George, a hawker, married Sarah, daughter of Lyon Levy, in 1838.*

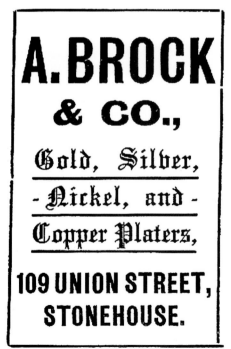

> *His son, Lewis Brock, a hairdresser, married Henrietta, daughter of Aaron Nathan the Plymouth constable, in 1860. In the 1871 census he [Lewis] describes himself as a musician. Indeed, later, together with his five sons, Henry, Charles, Alfred, Jacob Nathan (John) and Ernest, they were known locally as Brock's Band.*
>
> *Charles became a bookmaker with shares in a Plymouth nightclub and a clothing factory. By his will in 1947 he left some £25,000. Alfred, the first electro-plater in the West Country, had a jewelry shop and left £1,400. Ernest became wealthy. He was a partner with his brother and*

another in the clothing factory which employed several hundred people until it was destroyed in the Blitz; he was a bookmaker and he went into property. He was elected to the town council. When he died in 1950 he left £125,000. His widow, Lillian Ada, known as Cissie, a convert to Judaism and very proud of her new faith, also a town councillor and prominent in local affairs, carried on property business.[2]

The 1891 Census shows John Brock, occupation 'watchmaker', living with wife, Eva, a 'milliner', at 97 Union Street. In 1890 he had married Eva Lavinia K Atkins, the daughter of George and Mary Atkins. George had been the drill instructor with the Volunteers and lived at the Drill Grounds. Shortly afterwards Jacob Nathan changed his name to John, perhaps because his wife was not Jewish or because he wanted to assimilate himself more into the local community. The couple had two children: a daughter, Ivy Ernestine, born in 1894 and a son, Reginald Lewis, born four years later.

At the 1901 Census John Brock's family were living at 3, Marlborough Road, part of St Luke's parish, and his occupation is listed as 'Bicycle Dealer'. It is recorded that he also had a cycle shop in Ebrington Street at one time.[3] However, each ten-yearly census shows John Brock as being in Plymouth although he did spend time in other towns managing rinks before becoming manager of the Rinkeries in 1909.

A clue to his previous managerial posts can be found in an article which appeared in *The World's Fair*, a national magazine, in the early 1930s. A few of The Three Towns' rinks described earlier in Part One are also mentioned. It reads:

The history of the Millbay Rinkeries is an interesting one. Founded in the year 1909 by a company of enterprising private citizens, under the managership of Mr John Brock, it has had close upon 25 years of ever-increasing popularity. Mr Brock who, previous to his appointment to the above, was managerially connected with the newly-opened Plymouth Promenade Pier, might well be described as the pioneer of roller-skating – not only in Plymouth, but in the West.

Since his earliest days when he was in charge of the Albert Hall at Eldad, he has had an unlimited experience of both the sporting side and business side of the roller-skating art. Plymothians will well remember his activities at St Andrews Hall (which occupied the site of the present palatial General Post Office) and his strenuous endeavours to keep alive the pastime that at one time seemed on the point of dwindling out of existence. Subsequent to this, rinks were opened at Stonehouse under the name of the "Phoenix Hall" and in Martin Street, Plymouth, which everyone knows adjoins the famous Octagon. Mr Brock also opened and ran similar establishments in other Western towns, notably at Camborne and Liskeard.[4]

RINKERIES 1909 LIMITED

AMERICAN PALACE PIER

H. F. BLACKWELL
MANAGER

TO WHOM ALL COMMUNICATIONS SHOULD BE ADDRESSED

TELEPHONE № 370.
TELEGRAMS "PIER" St LEONARDS.

St LEONARDS ON SEA

AMERICAN PALACE PIER,
THE RENDEZVOUS OF ST. LEONARDS.

AMERICAN PALACE PIER
SKATING RINK.

THE MOST ELABORATE PAVILION
THEATRE, SEATING CAPACITY
OVER 800.

AMERICAN BOWLING ALLEYS

STEAMBOAT SERVICE DAILY.

WELL-APPOINTED RESTAURANT.
TEAS A SPECIALITY.

BRILLIANT ILLUMINATIONS.

FULL MILITARY BAND.

RINKERIES (1909) LTD.,
OPERATING
AMERICAN PALACE RINK,
ROYAL CONCERT HALL,
ST. LEONARDS.

ALDWYCH RINK, LONDON.

HIGHGATE RINK, HIGHGATE.

AMERICAN PALACE RINK,
PLYMOUTH.

VICTORIA PALACE RINK, EXETER.

TUNBRIDGE WELLS PALACE RINK,
TUNBRIDGE WELLS.

7th October, 09.

To Whom it may Concern.

This is to certify that Mr. J. Brock has been Floor Manager of our Rink for a considerable time, and that he leaves much against our will to take a more responsible position of one of our own Rinks, but if at any time there should be an opening in any of our establishments larger than the one he is to take charge of, I should hand him the responsibility which I am sure would be faithfully carried out.

MANAGER.

pro H. F. Blackwell

AMERICAN PALACE PIER.

146

Up to 1909 John Brock had been floor manager of the open air rink at St Leonards on Sea 'for some considerable time' but he had relinquished that post by the October to take up the managerial position at Millbay. A glowing testimonial was written for him by HF Blackwell, a director of Rinkeries 1909 Ltd. and manager of the American Palace Pier, St Leonards, where the rink was situated.

St Leonards' skaters, too, expressed their approval of Mr Brock's expertise at staging enjoyable events, one writing a letter to the local press that Brock *'had made the arrangements admirably for he is a capital man at this sort of thing'.*[5]

Supporters of the Millbay Rinkeries showed their appreciation of their manager by holding Benefit Nights for him. The first, held on 27th July 1910, was promoted in the local Press:

Next Wednesday a special benefit evening will be held for the manager, Mr J Brock. Mr Brock has shown himself a thorough business man during the period he has occupied the managerial chair, always catering for the comfort of his patrons, and doing all which laid in his power to make the Rink a thoroughly popular place of resort. Consequently, a large number of his admirers are expected at his benefit on Wednesday.[6]

The evening was a great success at which Master W Gaston, aged three, gave an exhibition of skating. The toddler also challenged anyone his own age to a Mile Race for a £100 prize. It was doubtful there were any takers! John Brock was presented with a travelling bag and his wife received a bouquet.[7]

Another successful Benefit Night was held for him on Thursday 13th July 1911. It is interesting to note that the programme invites those attending to 'come and see the Plan for the NEW SWIMMING BATH which is to be erected.'

Brock, in addition to being a superb organiser who staged numerous innovative attractions and diversions at Millbay, also sought to help his patrons in other ways, often giving out unusual prizes but ones which would be more than welcome. On Thursday 25th April 1912 he announced 'A Grand Provision Night' where 56 free prizes were awarded consisting of 20 cwts of coal, 12 hams, 60 lbs of lump sugar and 12 lbs of tea!

He was also a kind benefactor and supporter of local charities and national disaster funds. On the 18th November 1910 he held a benefit evening for the Ancient Order of Foresters, all proceeds going towards expenses incurred in entertaining the Foresters' High Court delegates in The Three Towns.

In 1912, following the terrible Titanic Disaster of the 15th April, Brock organised an 'Evening of Special Events', the programme stating: *REMEMBER: Every Patron on this evening is helping the Widows and Orphans of Brave Men, as the whole of the proceeds will be given to this Fund.*

On February 5th 1914 Brock held a 'Naval and Military Gymkhana' in aid of the A7 Submarine Disaster Fund at which the sum of £15 was raised. The tragedy, which shocked the Plymouth population, occurred on the 16th January when the A7 failed to surface in Whitsand Bay with the loss of all 11 men on board.[8]

Brock also gave his support to the Wrexham Miners' Relief Fund following the pit disaster there on 22nd September 1934. The explosion at the Gresford Colliery was one of the coal industry's worst and took 266 lives. Coming as it did so soon after the bitter industrial unrest of the 1920s it brought home to the nation just how perilous was the work of the coal miner. Brock, in conjunction with David Jordan of the Plymouth branch of the London Furnishing Company, promoted an evening of wrestling at which all those participating were awarded a silver medal. The programme shows John Brock aged 67.

John Brock gave his consent for the Rinkeries to be used for another fund-raising wrestling evening and on this occasion the bouts were in aid of the dependents of the HMS *Thetis* disaster which occurred at Holyhead on the 1st June 1939.

There were 103 men on board, twice the number she was allowed to carry. Of these 69 were crew and the rest were Cammell Laird engineers. One diver working on the outside of the ship and 99 men inside perished.[9] The 'Grand Star Wrestling Show' was presented at Millbay by Jack Bodinetz under the patronage of His Worship the Mayor of Plymouth and Admiral Sir E. Dunbar-Smith.

MILLBAY   RINKERIES

Proprietor: Mr. JOHN BROCK

OFFICIAL PROGRAMME

PRICE 2d.

Wrexham Miners' Relief Fund.

Under the Distinguished Patronage of—

THE EARL OF MOUNT EDGCUMBE,

Vice-Admiral SIR ERIC J. A. FULLERTON, K.C.B., D.S.O.M.A.,

Major L. HORE-BELISHA (Minister of Transport),

Captain The Hon. B. GUEST, C.B., D.S.O., M.P.,

Sir WILLIAM MOUNTSTEPHEN.

ORGANISED BY

Mr. JOHN BROCK, Proprietor of Millbay Rinkeries,

in conjunction with

Mr. DAVID JORDAN, of London Furnishing Co.

ALL NETT PROFITS GIVEN TO THE ABOVE FUND.

Chairs kindly lent by Plymouth Corporation.

Microphones and Amplifiers installed Free by the Parkside Amplifying Co., Plymouth.

GIFTS.

Onyx 3-Piece French Clock-Set by Mr. King Field, Jeweller, Courtenay Street, Plymouth.

4 Boxes of Chocolates by Mr. Francis, West Hoe Garage, Plymouth.

Valuable Picture by Mr. Bryant, 1, Hill Crescent, Mannamead, Plymouth.

J. H. Keys Ltd., Printers, Whimple St., Plymouth.

This postcard of the A7 submarine was published by Abrahams & Sons of Devonport.
(Julie Lawrence collection)

The Thetis, beached at Holyhead after the disaster in June 1939.
(Photo by Mackenzie J Gregory)

MILLBAY RINKERIES - PLYMOUTH

Wednesday, June 21st., 1939 at 8 p.m.

JACK BODINETZ PRESENTS A

GRAND STAR WRESTLING SHOW

Under the Patronage of His Worship the Mayor
of Plymouth and Admiral Sir E. Dunbar-Smith

In aid of the Dependents of "The Thetis" Disaster

SIX SENSATIONAL ALL-ACTION CONTESTS !

BLOCK D 4 **7/6**

Brock was also very community minded and in his *Cuttings Book* collected the calling cards of many of The Three Towns' elite. On March 12th 1910 he allowed Mrs Richard Trevithick to use the Rinkeries for an 'At Home'. It was a ticket only function lasting from 2.30 to 6.00pm with skating competitions and skates provided for the 100 guests. This successful 'At Home' was described in the local Press as *'an interesting innovation, which proves the popularity of skating among the middle and upper classes'* and the report also listed some of the guests.[10]

THIS CARD MUST BE GIVEN UP ON ENTRY.

Mr H. H. Wilcocks

Mrs. Trevithick

"At Home,"

The Rinkeries, Millbay,

Saturday, March 12th, 1910.

Skates provided.

R.S.V.P. before March 9th,
Penpol,
Lockyer Street,
Plymouth.

2.30 TO 6 P.M.

Skating Competitions.

On March 29th 1911 Brock organised a special prize draw for his skating clientele. Skaters attending that night would be given their admission or skate tickets in a sealed envelope and 16 of these would be marked 'Motor Trip'. The lucky tickets entitled winners to a free excursion – in £600 cars supplied by Humm & Co. – and an hour long stop for tea at Yelverton at a future date to be arranged, the whole expense to be defrayed by the management.

On Thursday 9th July 1914 Brock arranged the first River Trip and Dance at a cost of one shilling each. The *SS Brunel* left Millbay Docks at 6.15pm, North Corner at 6.45pm and Pottery Quay at 6.50. The Rinkeries Band was in attendance on the trip which landed at Pentillie. Permission for this had been obtained from W Coryton. After the outing the party was taken back to the Rinkeries for a dance lasting from 10.00pm until 12 midnight.

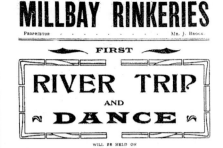

MILLBAY RINKERIES

PROPRIETOR · · · · · Mr. J. BROCK.

◆── FIRST ──◆

RIVER TRIP
AND
～ DANCE ～

WILL BE HELD ON

Thursday, July 9th, 1914

Per S.S. "BRUNEL,"

To PENTILLIE to land

(By kind permission of W. Coryton, Esq.)

Leaving MILLBAY DOCKS, 6-15 p.m.,
North Corner, 6-45, Pottery Quay, 6-50.

The Rinkeries Band will be in attendance.

After the Trip a **DANCE** will be held
at the Rink from 10 to 12.

Tickets, including Dance and River Trip, **1/-** each.

All Tickets must be obtained at the Rink or of any member of the
Hockey Club before the above date.

Seward, Mitchell & Co., Ltd., Buckland Hall, Plymouth.

Bedford Park Music and Dancing Academy.

Principals - Miss RUBY BAILEY, Mr. ROY JERRITT.

OPERATIC, GREEK, NATIONAL ACROBATIC
BALLET, BALLROOM AND STEP-DANCING
SINGING, PIANOFORTE, VIOLIN, 'CELLO
THEORY.

16 BEDFORD PARK,

TELEPHONE: PLYMOUTH 2571   PLYMOUTH, May 22nd, 1929.

Dear Mr. Brock,

On behalf of the Bedford Park Academy I wish to express
my thanks for the great kindness you showed Mr. and Mrs. Jerritt
and members of the Academy when you allowed them to visit and use
your bungalow at Newton Ferrers on Whit-Monday, and also for the
most enjoyable trip you gave them in your motor-boat.

The members of the Academy desire me to invite you to
become one of our Vice-Presidents, and I shall be extremely grate-
ful if you will accept. I would like to mention that our other
Vice-Presidents are The Rev. Herbert; Comdr. Hood; The Rev. J.
Roberton; Capt. Jerritt; and Mr. E. Watkins. Our President is
Mr. W. W. Jacobs.

I can assure you that Mr. and Mrs. Jerritt and the
students greatly appreciate your kindness.

Yours truly,

Hon. Sec.

J. Brock, Esq.,
    17, Athenaeum Street,
        Plymouth.

Surprisingly Brock's *Cuttings Book* holds far fewer press snippets and Rinkeries programmes after the Great War although there are a few boxing and wrestling flyers. This may have been because after 1913 he regularly leased out the Rinkeries to other individuals.

John Brock was a very valued member of the local community and did much to assimilate himself into public life. A letter dated 22nd May 1929 from the Bedford Park Music and Dancing Academy, based at 16 Bedford Park, thanked Brock for allowing their members to visit and use his bungalow at Newton Ferrers on Whit Monday. He had also given them a trip in his motor boat and as a result of his kindness the Academy invited him to become one of their Vice-Presidents.

The Newton Ferrers bungalow must have been Brock's second home for from around 1928, according to local directories, until his death in 1959 Brock resided at 17 Athenaeum Street, a fairly affluent address. John Brock passed away there in Plymouth on the 13th March at the grand old age of 91 and was buried in plot K25 of the Jewish Cemetery at Gifford Place.

Chapter Thirteen

World War Two – the end of an era

The extensive bombing which Plymouth endured in World War Two destroyed many fine buildings. The Victorian skating venues, although they had long been used for other businesses and activities, were among those which succumbed to the horrendous Blitz attacks, the first of which was delivered on the 6th July 1940. The worst onslaught began on the evening of Friday 21st March 1941 and continued until well after midnight.

Mill Bay Barracks and its Drill Hall, the venue for the very first roller rink in 1874, received a direct hit. Farley's Hotel was destroyed and the adjacent Buckland Hall went too.

The People's Palace in Martin Street, the Octagon, very near to the St James Hall, was another casualty in this area. Pat Twyford in his detailed account of the Blitz describes the scene:

The GPO building gutted by fire, 1941
(Chris Robinson collection)

Parts of Union Street were blasted and burnt into ruins, and there was one period when it seemed the entire Octagon was ringed with fire which engulfed Service & Co's premises and Jay's Furnishing Stores.[1]

The Royal Albert Hall at Eldad Hill was most certainly another victim as there is no trace of the premises there today. However, it was a miracle that the Palace Theatre, built on the site of the Phoenix Skating Rink, remained virtually unscathed.

Plymouth's General Post Office, which had incorporated the St Andrews Hall, was another casualty that night and the GPO was given new accommodation at Spears Corner, Tavistock Road.[2]

These two views show the twisted, burnt-out framework of the
Plymouth Promenade Pier, a poignant reminder of war
(Chris Robinson collection)

The stately Plymouth Pier, a treasured landmark for many Plymothians, was reduced to a burnt out shell, only the iron skeleton visible, standing starkly against the background of the Sound. It continued to be a reminder of that awful night until it was blown up and finally dismantled in 1953. Brian Moseley's excellent website gives the following account of its final disappearance:

> The blitzed remnants remained until the end of 1952. The City Council announced that they wanted it removed as soon as possible. There was no provision in the 'Plan for Plymouth' to rebuild the Pier. The War Damage Commission agreed to meet the cost of £4,754 and so a contract was placed with Messrs Eglinton Brothers of Plymouth for the demolition and removal of the ironwork under the supervision of engineers, Messrs G H Ivory & Partners. Work commenced in April 1953 and was to be completed by September 30th. Divers went down below the water to unbolt as many of the cross-members as they could before cutting off the ironwork that projected above water level. The Pier was built on iron columns embedded in the rock and these were removed by blasting.[3]

The Palladium Cinema in Ebrington Street, once the scene of so many cinderellas and carnivals at the American Skating Rink, was one of Plymouth's many picture houses to be hit.

The Millbay Rinkeries did not escape either. Attached as it was to the far end of the Ballard Institute which was completely destroyed it was left in a sorry state.

Films are silenced now at the Palladium. The film being shown was 'Songs and Bullets' (1938) starring Fred Scott (Chris Robinson collection

■ **The entrance to Millbay Rinkeries, with the Ballard Institute in the background**

Photo courtesy of the Evening Herald

The two night raids of the Blitz destroyed or damaged 20,000 properties at an estimated cost of around £100 million.[4]

But the carnage had far-reaching implications for future historical research. Many of Plymouth's municipal offices were wiped out together with much of the City's archival material.

Although the offices of the Western Morning News miraculously escaped, their photographic section on the opposite side of Frankfort Lane housing thousands of photographic records, negatives and prints, was completely burnt out.[5] This might explain why so few pictorial images remain of many of Plymouth's older Victorian buildings.

CHAPTER FOURTEEN

THE LAST YEARS OF ROLLER SKATING IN PLYMOUTH

Plymouth had no roller skating facilities for many years after the war although former skaters did look back on their rinking exploits with nostalgia. Ken Gardiner of Pennycross had fond memories of his daring escapades at the Rinkeries:

> I remember the Rinkeries all too well. Roller skating was a popular pastime in the thirties and was well patronised by the youngsters of the day. You had to be tough to survive there, I can assure you. Admission charge, if my memory serves me correctly, was sixpence. For that, you had the loan of skates and a couple of hours skating.

> The skates were secured to your footwear, mainly boots in those days, by clamps tightened on the soles by a key. When this was done, you made your way onto the floor of the rink with some trepidation. There was nothing sedate about the roller skating at Millbay Rinks, where recklessness was considered the norm and, I must confess, I was such a person. The wheels of the skates were of steel or fibre and the speedsters in the main preferred fibre as we were able to wet them which then gave better traction, allowing tighter turns and better manoeuvrability in speed.

> This proved helpful if you found yourself at the tail end of a snake, a snake being when you would hold the person-in-front's waist, shirt, come what may, and the leading skater would trail the hangers-on all over the rink, weaving from left to right at speed. Needless to say, in turning, those at the tail end where the most speed should be generated had to hang on for dear life, otherwise you were thrown out of control, invariably crashing into barriers.

> You had your thrills and chills and enjoyed it all. I wonder who's around today who has similar experiences at Millbay Rinks. You no doubt know the owners were the Brock family. A couple of them served as councillors, the best known being Cissy Brock who was at one time chairperson of the now defunct Watch Committee.[1]

David Fouracre of Peverell also wrote to the *Evening Herald* with memories of his rumbustious roller skating days at Millbay:

I went roller skating with some friends at Millbay Rinkeries. We never had our own skates at first. If you were a learner you stayed in the learner's rink and clung on to the rail on the wall. Often the new ones were terrorised by fast skaters deliberately buzzing past them at high speed. They did this for fun. It made some, especially the girls, even more timid to get their balance out in the rink and away from the wall.

I thought it was good fun and soon bought my own skates and key to tighten them on my boots and buckle a strap around the ankle, then, as an extra fastening you put rubber bands around the toe. These bands were car inner tubes cut up. I still have my skates! They've got steel rollers and were made in America.

I recall all those dangerous fast snake games they played, some would get a real battering yet they would recover and join on to the end of the snake again. I preferred just to go around the rink until on one occasion when I had not noticed a patch of the rink floor was wet. It had been raining and leaking through the roof. My skates slipped sideways and I couldn't save myself from crashing down!

They played nice music over the speakers, tunes that I remember now. The Skater's Waltz was played for couples who liked to dance together on skates.[2]

For a short period in the 1960s skating was provided at the old Forum Cinema at 110-112, Fore Street, Devonport. Advertised as that town's 'newest and latest cinema' it opened in 1938 with the film *'Broadway Melody'*.[3]

Although damaged during the Blitz it was repaired and continued to show films but by 1961 it had closed and all the cinema seats were removed. Films were replaced with boxing, wrestling and roller skating for a few years and there was some discussion in 1965 whether to turn the building into a much-needed local theatre. The venue is currently used for Bingo.[4]

In the late 1970s moves were made by Plymouth Ice Skating Club to establish an indoor ice rink either in Central Park or on a site in the area of Millbay Railway Station, this latter venue being the favourite.[5]

The cost of the venture was prohibitive and the Club's lottery to help finance the project folded after only six weeks.[6] The scheme was mooted again in 1988 but by this time the cost had doubled from £8.5 million to £17 million so again the project did not materialise.

Ice skating did take off in November 1981 at the 4,000 square feet synthetic ice rink opened by Bob Jones of Club West Ltd. at the Fiesta Skating Centre, Mayflower Street. Another rink, the Top Rank Skating Centre, was housed in part of the former Odeon Cinema in Union Street but, like the Fiesta, was short-lived.[7]

Roller skating surfaced again for a few years in 1981. Proposals for a rink were put to Plymouth's Planning Sub-committee and a report of that meeting appeared in the local Press

The Forum, Fore Street, Devonport
(Evening Herald/Guy Fleming)

under the heading 'Skating Into Jobs'. Alan Eagles intended to convert the 20,000 square feet of the former Ladybird clothing factory in Sutton Road, Coxside, which had been empty for 18 months, into a roller rink. The Sub-Committee had previously turned down a similar application on the grounds that they did not wish the location to pass into non-industrial use. However, Mr Eagles promised that more than 50 jobs could be provided – clerical and kitchen staff together with workers involved in roller skate manufacture – and he was advised to submit a fresh planning application.[8]

Despite much opposition from Labour and in particular Councillor Fred Johnson who declared 'teenagers, roller skating, liquor – it's the worst possible combination', his faction were defeated by 22 votes to 20 and the Coxside skating venue was approved.[9]

The Quayside Rollarena was officially opened at 6.20pm on Saturday 14th November 1981 by the Deputy Lord Mayor, John Pascoe. The building's refurbishment was carried out by a Milton Keynes firm with local sub-

Alan Eagles
(Midweek Independent)

contractors at a cost of £120,000 and had parking space for 70 vehicles. Like an earlier Plymouth skating venue it was described as an 'American-style rink' having a skating surface of 8,000 feet which was considered the biggest roller rink west of Bristol and probably in the whole of Britain.

The rink had its own skate shop and a workshop on the premises. It was open seven days a week – at lunchtimes from 12.30pm until 2.00pm and then from 2.30pm onwards – and admission prices were kept low. The standard admission fee was 50 pence with afternoon sessions costing 40 pence per head and school children could skate for 30 pence.[10]

Mr Eagles, who also had rinks in Wolverhampton and Milton Keynes, set out to make his establishment very family orientated, even providing a recreational area with ten pool tables and the latest video and pinball machines. A lengthy newspaper report described the proposed activities of the rink:

With lots of space, the best skates and expert help, Quayside Rollarena is expected to turn out Plymouth's future roller skating stars and will provide the city with some new excitement in speed skating and roller hockey.

Mr Eagles has broken up the evening sessions into short sessions. There is general skating; ladies speed skating; men's speed skating; then partners only skating under subdued lighting with a mirrored ball rotating from the ceiling.

Parents and friends can watch the children skating from the comfort of the ringside bar and restaurant. There is also a bar serving soft drinks and ice cream.

During every session, floor stewards control the skating to ensure that no one causes difficulties for the other skaters. No one must smoke or carry drinks onto the rink, scarves and hats cannot be worn and all skates are inspected to make sure they cannot cause any difficulties.

The report quotes Mr Eagles who describes activities very reminiscent of those at the Edwardian rinks:

'Mondays and Fridays are for over 21s. They can really let their hair down and enjoy themselves. There is usually a tug-o'-war on skates, musical dustbins, the giant see-saw, barrel jumping and long jump competitions. Sunday mornings are 'family mornings' when parents can skate with their children in a quiet atmosphere.'[11]

Another diversion was the on-stage DJ, known only by his first name 'Nigel', who frequently went onto the rink and skated around with a hand-held mike talking to skaters whose conversations were relayed back through the broadcasting system.

A rink professional, Mr Patrick Francey, was employed to coach skaters who would then take National Skating Association tests. Dancing competitions were arranged, these all-day events to take place on Sundays. Eagles also hoped to include skating as part of the school curriculum, a system introduced at his other venues, and discounts were offered to local schools and youth clubs.

Eagles, who at the time was Vice-President of the National Roller Hockey Association, was also keen to promote speed skating and roller hockey by offering free training time at the rink. He already had two under-13's teams from his Milton Keynes rink representing Great Britain and hoped to form hockey teams in Plymouth and the West Country to compete in national league matches.

The Rollarena's hockey teams consisting of two over 16's and two under 16's, a total of 45 players, were run by Harry Hartnett and Cliff Collingwood. The Sport's Council had generously given a £1,000 grant to get them started.[12]

Eagles, who had skated since boyhood, became involved in the roller skating business in 1966, opening his first rink at Wolverhampton in 1968 and another at Milton Keynes shortly afterwards. He had designed his own Eagle Olympic skates, which sold at £37.20 per pair and had a lifetime guarantee, and he planned to use the repair workshops installed at the Rollarena to manufacture the Eagle skates at Cattedown.[13]

The rink appears to have been very successful for a few years with midweek attendances of 250 per night, doubling at weekends. However, the last of Plymouth's skating rinks was to last just six years before it went into liquidation. It had been a popular venue for children's parties and the home of four roller hockey teams but it closed abruptly without prior notice leaving youngsters bereft and the hockey players without a venue. The rink had suffered a 40 per cent drop in trade up to its sudden closure in November 1987 and Managing Director, Mr Eagles, had no alternative but to wind up the business.[14]

The closure left hundreds of young people with nowhere to skate and their parents irate, some believing that lack of support was due to poor publicity. Scores of angry roller skaters planned a protest march on Sunday November 22nd, skating from the Hoe to the Rollarena. The local Press described this 'Demo on wheels against closure of roller rink':

> *A protest against the closure of Plymouth's Rollarena skating rink was hailed as 'a great success'. Scores of skaters mounted a demonstration on wheels to the doomed venue in Coxside. Organiser Ann Marks said: 'We proved that there is a demand for a roller rink in Plymouth.'*
>
> *The angry roller fans skated from Plymouth Hoe through the city centre. They pinned a sign on the rink's closed doors which read: 'Entrepreneur required to re-open this venue urgently.'*
>
> *Mrs Marks has been approached by a businessman interested in forming a consortium to revive the roller venue.*
>
> *Heather Collins, 8, and Wayne Neal, 10, who were to have celebrated their birthdays at a Rollerena party on Sunday, took part in the protest.*
>
> *The Rollerena closed ten days ago after a sharp fall in custom.[15]*

Despite this protest march and the vague promise of financial backing the rink did not survive. Auctioneers Fieldens of Plymouth arranged a clearance auction of roller skates, catering and bar equipment, 'on instructions from the Sheriff of Devon', at the Rollerena on the 24th November 1987. A list of the skating equipment to be sold at this public auction is given in Appendix XIII.

Plymouth's 115 years of roller skating history ends on a final sad note. In September 1989 David Gibbs, whose mobile rent-a-rink travelled throughout West Devon and Cornwall, was appealing for a suitable Plymouth location to install his portable plywood rink. Gibbs had been manager at the Coxside Rollarena since its inception and Alan Eagles helped him set up the enterprise.

Roller rink closes down

PLYMOUTH Rollerena has closed following a dramatic slump in trade during the past year.

Last minute talks to save the roller rink in Sutton Road, Coxside, have failed.

Managing director Alan Eagles said : "It is a very sad day for me, but I just could not keep it open as things were."

He blamed reductions in bus services past the arena for the dwindling number of customers.

Mr Eagles opened the Rollerena in 1981 in a disused clothing factory.

Evening Herald
13th November 1987

Demo on wheels against closure of roller rink

by TERRY MESSENGER

A PROTEST against the closure of Plymouth's Rollarena skating rink was hailed as "a great success".

Scores of skaters mounted a demonstration on wheels to the doomed venue in Coxside.

Organiser Ann Marks said: "We proved that there is a demand for a roller rink in Plymouth."

The angry roller fans skated from Plymouth Hoe through the city centre.

They pinned a sign on the rink's closed doors which read: "Entrepreneur required to re-open this venue urgently."

Birthdays

Mrs Marks has been approached by a businessman interested in forming a consortium to revive the roller venue.

Heather Collins, 8, and Wayne Neal, 10, who were to have celebrated their birthdays at a Rollarena party on Sunday, took part in the protest.

The Rollarena closed ten days ago after a sharp fall in custom.

Evening Herald, Tuesday, November 24, 1987

THE JOYS OF ROLLER SKATING BUT NOWHERE TO GO

Evening Herald
24th November 1987

165

Gibbs transported skates for 300 youngsters around the South West in his Ford Transit van and his rink could also be set up for fetes or private functions. He also hoped to run skating sessions during the winter months at the Mayflower Sports Centre but with five-a-side football held there six nights a week there was no room for roller skating, nor any other sports.[16]

The only existing skating venue is currently to be found at the synthetic ice rink at the Pavilions Leisure Complex which opened in September 1991. With talk of the demolition of Plymouth Pavilions as part of the refurbishment plans for Millbay who knows how long skating will last here.

Skating is still the only fun pastime and healthy exercise which can be undertaken *en masse.* But it is sad that there are now few opportunities to indulge in the sport.

This valuable fitness routine seems to have been replaced in the 21st century by sessions at the gym, swimming, cycling and skateboarding – but that's another story ...

FULL PAY OF THE ROYAL NAVY.

§ III. WAGES TABLE—SHIP'S COMPANY, &c.

APPENDIX I

NAVY LIST 1875

Distinguishing No.	Ratings	Continuous Service — Year of 365 Days (£ s. d.)	One Day (s. d.)	Non-continuous Service — Year of 365 Days (£ s. d.)	One Day (s. d.)
1	Able Seaman	28 17 11	1 7	24 6 8	1 4
·	Admiral's Cook, 1st Class Domestic*	…	…	28 17 11	1 8
3	Ditto Coxswain—				
	Under 3 Years' Service as Chief Petty Officer	47 2 11	2 7	42 11 8	2 4
	Over 3 Years' Service as Chief Petty Officer	50 3 9	2 9	45 12 6	2 6
4	Ditto Domestic, 1st Class Domestic*	48 13 4	2 8	44 2 1	2 5
5	Ditto Steward, 1st Class Domestic*	30 8 4	1 8	25 17 1	1 5
6	Armourer				
7	Armourer's Crew				
8	Assistant Baker, in Troop Ships, 3rd Class Domestic*	24 6 8	1 4	19 15 5	1 1
9	Assistant Sick Berth Attendant*			24 6 8	1 4
10	Baker, in Troop Ships, 2nd Class Domestic*	24 6 8	1 4	24 6 8	1 4
11	Bandmaster††	34 19 7	1 11	34 19 7	1 11
12	Bandsman††	24 6 8	1 4	24 6 8	1 4
13	Bandsman, 2nd Class*††	22 16 8	1 3	22 16 8	1 3
14	Band Boy*	10 2 11	0 7		
15	Barber				
16	Blacksmith	48 13 4	2 8	44 2 1	2 5
17	Blacksmith's Crew	30 8 4	1 8	25 17 1	1 5
18	Boatswain's Mate	39 10 10	2 2	34 19 7	1 11
19	Boy, 1st Class*	10 2 11	0 7		
20	Boy, 2nd Class*	9 2 6	0 6		
21	Boy Writer*	18 5 0	1 0		
22	Butcher				
23	Captain of Quarter-deck Men	39 10 10	2 2	34 19 7	1 11
24	Captain of the Forecastle	39 10 10	2 2	34 19 7	1 11
25	Captain of the Foretop	39 10 10	2 2	34 19 7	1 11
26	Captain of the Hold	39 10 10	2 2	34 19 7	1 11
27	Captain of the Maintop	39 10 10	2 2	34 19 7	1 11
28	Captain of the Mast	34 19 7	1 11	30 8 4	1 8
29	Captain of the Mizentop	34 19 7	1 11	30 8 4	1 8
30	Captain's Cook, in all rated Ships, 1st Class Domestic*	…	…	28 17 11	1 7
31	Captain's Cook, in Ships below 6th Rates, 2nd Class Domestic*	…	…	24 6 8	1 4
32	Captain's Cook's Assistant, 3rd Class Domestic*	…	…	19 15 5	1 1
33	Captain's Coxswain	39 10 10	2 2	34 19 7	1 11
34	Captain's Servant, 2nd Class Domestic*	24 6 8	1 4	19 15 5	1 1
35	Captain's Steward, in all rated Ships, 1st Class Domestic*	…	…	28 17 11	1 8

* Not entitled to Good Conduct Pay or Badges.
†† C.S. If trained up in the service from Band Boy.

FULL PAY OF THE ROYAL NAVY. 1875

§ III. WAGES TABLE—SHIP'S COMPANY, &c.—continued.

Ratings	Continuous Service — Year of 365 Days (£ s. d.)	One Day (s. d.)	Non-continuous Service — Year of 365 Days (£ s. d.)	One Day (s. d.)
(Captain's Steward, in Ships below) 6th Rates, 2nd Class Domestic*	…	…	24 6 8	1 4
Carpenter's Crew, 2nd Class*	34 19 7	1 11	30 8 4	1 8
Carpenter's Mate	22 16 8	1 8	45 12 …	2 6
Caulker	50 8 9	2 9	45 12 6	2 6
Caulker's Mate	41 9	2 3	36 10	2 0
Chief Bandmaster††	39 10 10	2 3	36 10	2 2
Chief Boatswain's Mate—				
Under 3 Years' Service as Chief Petty Officer	47 2 11	2 7	42 11 8	2 4
Over 3 Years' Service as Chief Petty Officer	50 3 9	2 9	45 12 6	2 6
Chief Captain of the Forecastle—				
Under 3 Years' Service as Chief Petty Officer	47 2 11	2 7	42 11 8	2 4
Over 3 Years' Service as Chief Petty Officer	50 3 9	2 9	45 12 6	2 6
Chief Carpenter's Mate	51 15 0	3 0	50 3 9	2 9
Chief Gunner's Mate—				
Under 3 Years' Service as Chief Petty Officer	47 2 11	2 7	42 11 8	2 4
Over 3 Years' Service as Chief Petty Officer	50 3 9	2 9	45 12 6	2 6
Chief Quartermaster—				
Under 3 Years' Service as Chief Petty Officer	47 2 11	2 7	42 11 8	2 4
Over 3 Years' Service as Chief Petty Officer	50 3 9	2 9	45 12 6	2 6
Chief Yeoman of Signals—				
Under 3 Years' Service as Chief Petty Officer	47 2 11	2 7	42 11 8	2 4
Over 3 Years' Service as Chief Petty Officer	50 3 9	2 9	45 12 6	2 6
Commander's Servant, 2nd Class Domestic*	…	…	24 6 8	1 4
Cook's Mate [Entered under Order in Council of 9th Aug., 1872.*] 1st Class / 2nd Class	28 17 11 / 22 16 3	1 7 / 1 3	19 15 …	1 1
Cook's Mate* (old system)	45 12 6	2 6	41 1 1	2 3
Cooper*	30 8 4	1 8	25 17 1	1 5
Cooper's Crew	34 19 7	1 11	30 8 4	1 8
Coxswain of the Barge	34 19 7	1 11	30 8 4	1 8
Coxswain of the Cutter	34 19 7	1 11	30 8 4	1 8

* Not entitled to Good Conduct Pay or Badges.
†† C.S. If trained up in the service from Band Boy.

APPENDIX II

The following table shows a sample of dock wages for 1875 set alongside **Barnsby's Scales** for 1875-79 and **Wood's Index** for the average male wage for those years.

DOCKYARD WAGES 1875   EQUAL TO

LOOK-OUT MEN	*2s 6d per day x 7*	*17s 6d per week*
BOILERMAKERS		
	6s 0d per day x 6	*£1 16s 0d per week*
	rising to	
	9s 0d per day x 6	*£2 14s 0d per week*
SHIPWRIGHTS		
	6s 0d per day x 6	*£1 16s 0d per week*
	rising to	
	11s 0d per day x 6	*£3 6s 0d per week*
LEADING DRAUGHTSMEN		
	10s 0d per day x 6	*£3 0s 0d per week*

1875-1879

BARNSBY'S MINIMUM COMFORT STANDARD	*£1 12s 9d per week*
BARNSBY'S DEEP POVERTY LEVEL	*£1 2s 6d per week*
BARNSBY'S SUBSISTENCE LEVEL	*13s 3d per week*
WOOD'S INDEX AVERAGE MALE WAGE	*£1 4s 9d per week*

It is apparent from the above figures that dock workers' weekly wages were above the average for males stated in *Wood's Index* to which Barnsby refers and, except for 'look-out men', exceeded *Barnsby's Scale* for 'minimum comfort level'. Moreover, dockyard employment, in addition to being well paid, was relatively secure.

APPENDIX III

DOCKYARD WORKING HOURS 1877

Dockyard Circular No. 22 D, of 25th July, 1877).

TABLE of Working Hours for the Work-people at the Spinning and Ropery Departments, and for the Colour Women, in Her Majesty's Dockyards.

Period of the Year.	Workpeople to enter the Yard	Work to Commence.	Stop for Breakfast.	Re-commence Work.	Stop for Dinner.	Work to Commence.	Stop for Cleaning Machines.	To Change Clothing.	Cease Work for Closing Windows.	To Leave the Building.	Hours worked Daily.	Hours worked Weekly.	Average Number of Hours worked Daily.
	h.m.	h.m.	h.m.	h.m.	h.m.	h.m.	h.m.	h.m.	h.m.	h.m.	h.m.	h.m.	
January	7.45	7.57	..	..	12.0	12.30	9.40	3.50	3.55	4.0	7.33	42.48	
February	7.30	7.42	..	.	12.0	12.30	4.28	4.38	4.43	4.48	8.36	48.18	
March 1st to September 30th ..	6.48	7.0	9.0	9.30	1.0	1.30	5.40	5.50	5.55	6.0	10.0	56.3	
October	7.30	7.42	..	..	12.0	12.30	4.28	4.38	4.43	4.48	8.36	48.18	
November 1st to 15th	7.30	7.42	..	..	12.0	12.30	3.43	3.53	3.58	4.3	7.51	44.33	
November 16th to December 31st	7.45	7.57	..	..	12.0	12.30	3.25	3.35	3.40	3.45	7.18	41.33	h.m. >8.31¼
Saturdays throughout the year. Mornings in accordance with the above Periods			Refreshment				1.0	1.10	1.15	1.20	..	..	
			11.0	11.30	..	..							

Appendix IV

A Brief Chronology of Local Railways
1818-1971

1818   Sir Thomas Tyrwitt proposes Plymouth & Dartmoor Tramway

1821   Leigham Tunnel constructed

1823   Plymouth & Dartmoor Tramway opens

1834   Plympton Extension

1847   Plympton branch of P&D sold to South Devon Railway to allow main line into Plymouth by construction of Skew Bridge

1848   Laira Green station opens the first main line station

1849   Millbay Station opens; Laira Green closes

1850   Millbay Docks open

1853   Lee Moor Tramway construction starts. Sutton harbour branch opens

1858   Lee Moor Tramway

1859   GWR opens Plymouth to Cornwall service across the Brunel Bridge; Plymouth to Tavistock line opens; Devonport (Albert Road)

1861   Marsh Mills station

1867   Dockyard Railway opens and connects to main line at Keyham

1871   Mutley Station

1876   Devonport Kings Road opens LSWR - trains arrive via Lydford, Tavistock, Marsh Mills. Cornwall Loop opens

1877   Stonehouse pool line opens (LSWR Ocean Terminal). North Road station opens

1879   Cattewater branch line

1883   Princetown to Yelverton line

1890   St Budeaux (Victoria Road) opens; Devonport Kings Road converted to through station

1891   Friary Station

1892   Laira Bridge

1898   Billacombe, Elburton, Brixton and Yealmpton stations opened

1900   Keyham Station opens

1904   Laira Halt, Lipson Vale Halt, Wingfield Villas Halt, Ford Halt and St Budeaux (Ferry Road) all opened

1905   Mount Gould, Tothill Halt and Dockyard Halt open

1906	Weston Mill Halt, Camel's Head Halt, Albert Road Halt and Plym Bridge platform all opened
1918	Mount Gould and Tothill Halt close
1921	Wingfield Villas and Weston Mill Halts close
1930	Laira Halt closes 1939 Mutley Station closes
1941	Millbay closes to passengers; Ford Halt closes
1942	Lipson Vale and Camel's Head Halts close
1947	Albert Halt closed; Yealmpton Branch and all its stations close
1951	Turnchapel branch closes to passengers
1956	Princetown to Yelverton line closes
1958	Friary closes to passengers
1959	Plympton station closes
1961	Plymstock to Turnchapel closed to goods
1962	Line between Tavistock and Launceston and all stations close
1964	Devonport Kings Road closed to passengers
1969	Sutton Harbour branch closes
1971	Devonport Kings Road closed to goods

APPENDIX V – PLIMPTON'S SKATE PATENT 25TH AUGUST, 1865

A.D. 1865, *25th August*. N° 2190.

Skates.

LETTERS PATENT to Alfred Vincent Newton, of the Office for Patents, 66, Chancery Lane, in the County of Middlesex, Mechanical Draughts-man, for the Invention of "IMPROVEMENTS IN THE CONSTRUCTION OF SKATES."—A communication from abroad by James Leonard Plumpton, of the City of New York, in the United States of America.

Sealed the 9th January 1866, and dated the 25th August 1865.

PROVISIONAL SPECIFICATION left by the said Alfred Vincent Newton at the Office of the Commissioners of Patents, with his Petition, on the 25th August 1865.

I ALFRED VINCENT NEWTON, of the Office for Patents, 66, Chancery Lane, 5 in the County of Middlesex, Mechanical Draughtsman, do hereby declare the nature of the said Invention for "IMPROVEMENTS IN THE CONSTRUCTION OF SKATES," to be as follows :—

This Invention relates to an improvement in attaching the rollers or runners to the stock or foot stand of the skate, whereby the rollers or runners are 10 made to turn or cant by the rocking of the stock or foot stand, and thus facilitate the turning of the skate on the ice or floor, and admit of the skater performing with ease gyrations or evolutions without taxing unduly the muscles of the foot or ankles. On the under face of the skate stock are affixed two plates of peculiar construction, the one at the toe and the other at

Newton's Improvements in the Construction of Skates.

the heel. These plates are similarly formed with a socket near the stock, and they terminate in a journal which takes a downward inclined direction. The socket receives the end of a longitudinal bar which is formed at its other end into a socket to receive the journal forming the termination of the fixed plate. This longitudinal bar is a portion of a casting which may be termed a hanger, 5 it being provided with four horns for receiving the axle for a pair of rollers, which rollers are to be roughed with emery or otherwise on their periphery. The hanger is secured to the fixed plate by a vertical screw, which passes through a block of india-rubber, interposed between the head of the screw and the hanger. Allowance is thus made for the oscillation of the hanger and the 10 wheels which it carries, and to limit this inclines are made on the fixed plates to act as stops when the desired limit is reached. The axle of the rollers is secured in position by a sliding key, which slides down one of the horns and passes through one end of the axle. When runners are used in place of rollers they are held in pairs of clamps which are secured to the axle, and 15 collars of india-rubber are slipped on the axle to form elastic supports to the clamps, and allow them to yield to facilitate the performance of evolutions upon the ice. To check an undue lateral movement of the clamps they are formed with projections which will bear against the sides of the hanger when the limit allowed is reached. The runners are made with straight parallel 20 angular edges and admit of being reversed in the clamps when one edge is worn.

SPECIFICATION in pursuance of the conditions of the Letters Patent, filed by the said Alfred Vincent Newton in the Great Seal Patent Office on the 24th February 1866.   25

TO ALL TO WHOM THESE PRESENTS SHALL COME, I, ALFRED VINCENT NEWTON, of the Office for Patents, 66, Chancery Lane, in the County of Middlesex, Mechanical Draughtsman, send greeting.

WHEREAS Her most Excellent Majesty Queen Victoria, by Her Letters Patent, bearing date the Twenty-fifth day of August, in the year of our Lord 30 One thousand eight hundred and sixty-five, in the twenty-ninth year of Her reign, did, for Herself, Her heirs and successors, give and grant unto me, the said Alfred Vincent Newton, Her special licence that I, the said Alfred Vincent Newton, my executors, administrators, and assigns, or such others as I, the said Alfred Vincent Newton, my executors, administrators, and assigns, 35

should at any time agree with, and no others, from time to time and at all times thereafter during the term therein expressed, should and lawfully might make, use, exercise, and vend, within the United Kingdom of Great Britain and Ireland, the Channel Islands, and Isle of Man, an Invention for
5 " IMPROVEMENTS IN THE CONSTRUCTION OF SKATES," being a communication from abroad, upon the condition (amongst others) that I, the said Alfred Vincent Newton, my executors or administrators, by an instrument in writing under my, or their, or one of their hands and seals, should particularly describe and ascertain the nature of the said Invention, and in what manner the
10 same was to be performed, and cause the same to be filed in the Great Seal Patent Office within six calendar months next and immediately after the date of the said Letters Patent.

NOW KNOW YE, that I, the said Alfred Vincent Newton, do hereby declare the nature of the said Invention, and in what manner the same is
15 to be performed, to be particularly described and ascertained in and by the following statement, reference being had to the Drawing hereunto annexed, and to the letters and figures marked thereon (that is to say) :—

This Invention relates to an improvement in attaching the rollers or runners to the stock or foot stand of the skate, whereby the rollers or runners are
20 made to turn or cant by the rocking of the stock or foot stand, so as to assume radii of a circle and facilitate the turning of the skate on the ice or floor, and admit of the skater performing with ease gyrations or revolutions without taxing unduly the muscles of the foot or ankles.

In the accompanying Drawing, Fig. 1 represents a side view of a parlor or
25 roller skate applied to the foot; Fig. 2 is a bottom or under view of the same ; Fig. 3 is an under view of a plate pertaining to the same ; Fig. 4, a side view of a roller pertaining to the same with its outside bearing and catch or fastening for holding it on its shaft ; Fig. 5 is a section of Fig. 4, taken in the line x, x; Fig. 6 is a side view of the front part of the skate with runners
30 attached ; Fig. 7 is a bottom or under view of Fig. 6 ; Fig. 8 is a section of Fig. 7 taken in the line y, y; Fig. 9 is a detached inner side view of a plate pertaining to the runners of the skate ; Fig. 10 is a transverse vertical section of Fig. 2, taken in the line z, z; Fig. 11 is a transverse vertical section of Fig. 2, taken in the line z^1, z^1 ; and Fig. 12 is a diagram showing the position
35 as secured by the rollers or runners in turning a curve ; Fig. 13 is a longitudinal section taken in the line z^2, z^2, of Fig. 2. Similar letters of reference indicate corresponding parts. A represents the stock or foot stand of the skate which may be constructed in any proper manner, and B, B, represent the metal

plates, which are firmly secured to the under side of the stock or foot stand, one near the toe, and the other at the heel of the same. These plates B, B, are of triangular form, see Fig. 3, and may be secured to the stock or foot stand by a screw a, one near each angle or corner. At the angular end of each plate B, there is a socket b, and from the socket of each plate there extends longitudi- 5 nally and centrally an inclined ledge b^1, the outer end of which is rounded to form a journal c, shown clearly in Fig. 3, and at the broad ends of the plates B, B, there are pendent projections d, d, which are shown clearly in Figures 10 and 11. These plates it will be seen by referring to Figure 1, are secured to the stock or foot stand in opposite positions, so that the inclined ledges b, b, will 10 extend down from the front and rear ends of the same towards a point in a vertical line passing about through the centre of the stock, or foot stand. C, C, represent what may be termed the hangers, the same being composed of four inclined pendent bars e, e, e^1, e^1, extending down from a bar f, having a bar g crossing it at right angles. The bars g have at one end a 15 journal to fit into a socket of the plates B, B, and the opposite ends of the bars g are provided with sockets i, to receive the journals c of said plates B. This arrangement admits of the stock or foot stand having a lateral tilting movement either to the right or left. In the lower parts of the inclined pendent bars e, e, e^1, e^1, of each hanger c, there is inserted a shaft D, on which 20 rollers E are placed so as to turn loosely. This shaft has a head at one end and a sliding key F passes through the opposite end, which key is flattened at one part sufficiently to admit of an oblong slot j (see Fig. 4) being made longitudinally through it to allow a pin k, in one of the bars e to pass through the said pin k, serving as a guide for the key. The key is prevented from 25 casually drawing out from the hole in shaft D by having a slot l, see Fig. 4, at the outer end of slot j, at right angles to it, in which slot l the pin k may be fitted, and the key F is prevented from being shoved laterally so as to prevent the pin k from casually getting out of l, by means of a button G, which is fitted on the pin k, and has a flange in it at one end to fit over the side of 30 F. When the key is to be withdrawn from the hole in shaft D to admit of the removal of the latter, the button G is turned so that its flange m will be at the outer end of the key F, and admit of the key F being shoved laterally, so that the pin k may be adjusted in the slot j, and admit of a longitudinal movement of the key. By this arrangement the shafts D are firmly secured 35 in the hangers, and at the same time may be readily removed therefrom when necessary or required. The rollers E are placed on the shafts between the arms e, e^1, e, e^1, as shewn in Fig. 2, and their peripheries are covered with

Newton's Improvements in the Construction of Skates.

emery or have a roughened surface produced in any proper way in order to prevent them from slipping. The hangers C, C, are secured to the plates B, B, by screws n, which pass through the centre of the bars g of the hangers and into the inclined ledges b, b, of the plates B, said screws having a plate o
5 on them, between which and the bars g a spring p of india-rubber or other suitable material is placed. These springs p keep the hangers in contact with the plates B and prevent all unnecessary play or vibration of the same in an upward direction, and control the turning, tilting, or canting of the stock or foot stand. In consequence of the ledges b, b, of the plates B, B, being
10 inclined, it will be seen that if the stock or foot stand A be tilted or inclined either to the right or left, the shaft hangers C, C, and consequently the shafts D, will be cramped so as to form radii of a circle, see Fig. 12, and the skate will consequently move in or describe a curve. The skater, therefore has perfect command over the skates, and is enabled to perform curves, gyrations,
15 and evolutions with the greatest facility.

When the Invention is to be used on ice, runners are employed, constructed and applied as follows:—Upon the shafts D there are placed loosely what may be termed clamps H, composed of two parts q, r. The parts q may be of any ornamental design (that of a swan is here represented) and the other
20 part r is simply a plate secured to q by a screw s, the runner I being between q, r. The runners I, have smooth running surfaces with angular edges, so that they may be reversed when the inner edges lose their angularity by wear and a fresh sharp edge obtained, and when both edges of one surface become worn the runner may be inverted, and two more angular or sharp edges
25 obtained. Thus each runner has four angular edges which may be successively used before the runner will require to be sharpened. The clamps H are retained in proper position on the shafts D by india-rubber or other washers J, shown clearly in Fig. 7. The stock or foot stand is prevented from tilting beyond a proper distance in consequence of the bars f of the hangers coming
30 in contact with the pendent projections d, d, of the plates B, B, while the clamps H on the shafts D have their movement thereon limited by the ends of the wings of the swan and the tail coming in contact with the bars f.

Under the above in part recited Letters Patent I claim,—

35 First, applying rollers or runners to the stock or foot stand of a skate, as described, so that the said rollers or runners may be cramped or turned so as to cause the skate to run in a curved line either to the right or left by the turning, canting, or tilting laterally of the stock or foot stand.

Newton's Improvements in the Construction of Skates.

Second, the mode of securing the runners and making them reversible as above-described.

In witness whereof I, the said Alfred Vincent Newton, have hereunto set my hand and seal, the Twenty-fourth day of February, in the year of our Lord One thousand eight hundred and sixty-six.   5

A. V. NEWTON. (L.S.)

Witness,
    J. W. MOFFATT,
        66, Chancery Lane.

LONDON:
Printed by GEORGE EDWARD EYRE and WILLIAM SPOTTISWOODE,
Printers to the Queen's most Excellent Majesty   1866.

2 AU 66

Appendix VI – Plimpton's Skate Design – Original Drawings 1865

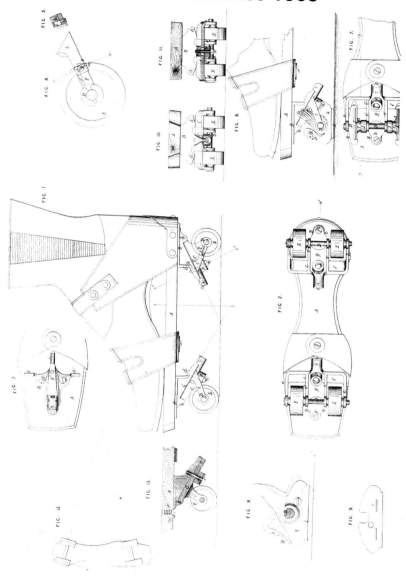

Joh]

ALPHABETICAL INDEX OF PATENTEES AND

[Juv

Name	Number of Application.	Date of Application.	Subject.
Johnston, J. B.	2259	May 29	Checks; money-orders, &c.
Johnston, J. L. (Auld)	4782	Dec. 11	Preparing and combining substances for food.
„ S. (Lake)	1555	Apr. 12	Binding wheat sheaves, &c.
„ S. (Lake)	1822	May 1	Harvesting-machines.
„ S. (Lake)	2795	July 8	Reaping-machines.
Johnston, T.	2683	June 29	Golf-clubs.
Johnston Harvester Co. (Vaughan)	145	Jan. 13	Reaping and harvesting machines.
„ Harvester Co. (Vaughan)	2673	June 28	Binding grain.
Johnstone, J.	2416	June 12	School desks and seats.
Johnstone, J. J., & Straiton, J.	185	Jan. 18	Cleaning skins.
Joliessaint-Vonéche, & La Société Comité [§ Mabut (Tongue)	1476	Apr. 6	Textile leather.
Jones, A. W., & Chamberlain, H.	2865	July 13	Solitaires and studs.
„ D.	4431	Nov. 16	Stopping or retarding railway trains.
„ E. A. & J. A.	3952	Oct. 12	Making iron and steel.
„ F. W.	3083	Aug. 2	Indicating if closets or rooms are engaged, &c.
„ Harry E.	1063	Mar. 11	Regulating, &c. pressure of gas.
„ Harry, Langston-	1682	Apr. 21	Disinfectants and deodorisers.
„ Henry, & Cook, E.	3555	Sep. 11	Rolling hoop-iron.
„ Hugh, & Lewis, J.	928	Mar. 4	Roller skates.
„ J., Thomas, D., Williams, D., [& Jenkins, J.	1120	Mar. 15	Utilising old annealing pots of tin-plate works.
„ J. A. & E. A.	3952	Oct. 12	Making iron and steel.
„ J. G.	793	Feb. 25	Boring and breaking down coal, &c.
„ J. G.	3573	Sep. 12	Indicating speed of ships' railway carriages,&c.
„ M. P.	917	Mar. 3	Rink or parlour skates.
Jones, O. (Lake)	2777	July 7	Revolving cylinder pistols.
Jones, P.	2575	June 22	Blankets.
„ R. J.	2809	July 10	Clog-blocks.
„ T. H., & Ellis, G.	1421	Apr. 3	Dressing slates.
„ W.	1055	Mar. 11	Sewing-machines.
Jordan, L.	481	Feb. 7	Pumps and beer-engines.
„ T. R.	2719	July 1	Roller skates.
Jouve, L. Z. (Vaughan)	1263	Mar. 25	Sugar-making.
Jowett, G., & Rushworth, C.	3136	Aug. 8	Bottle-stoppers and securing same.
„ J.	3913	Oct. 10	Preventing rattling of windows, &c.
„ J., & Sergeant, J.	2188	May 24	Combing fibres.
„ J., & Wood, E.	3242	Aug. 17	Boiler-furnace and other doors.
Joy, D.	4707	Dec. 5	Motive-power engines.
Joyce, A. E.	1962	May 10	Roller skates.
„ R. J. S., & Weintraud, F.	3436	Aug. 31	Solitaires and studs.
Jubber, H.	4740	Dec. 7	Raising sunken ships, &c.
Judge, J.	2798	July 8	Railway signals.
„ J.	4891	Dec. 4	Signalling to drivers of locomotives.
„ J., & Haslam, L.	4798	Dec. 12	Making horse-shoes.
„ T.	2990	July 24	Cases for storage, &c. of explosives.
Judson, E.	4569	Nov. 25	Explosive compounds.
Julion-Sauve, H., & Krafft, L.	4976	Dec. 23	Treating iron, Bessemer, Martin, and other [metals for forming into steel.
Jullien, A. (Browne)	4495	Nov. 21	Metallic alloys of iron, &c.
„ A. (Ledger)	4499	Nov. 21	Making cast steel and hardening same.
Jullien, E., & Curré, F. P. E.	3594	Sep. 13	Refrigerating-apparatus.
Juned-Pattus, A. L. (Clark)	2797	July 8	Keyless repeating watches.
Juron, C. (Johnson)	2684	June 29	Cocks.
Justice, P. S.	1077	Mar. 11	Cases for covering objects.
„ P. S.	4757	Dec. 3	Extinguishing sparks and condensing exhaust [steam in engines.
„ P. S. (Shaw)	234	Jan. 20	Steam-engines; steam and vacuum brakes.
„ P. S. (Mason)	4641	Nov. 30	Sewing-machine embroidery attachment.
Juvenal, J.M., & Gravot,P.A.(Brewer)	61	Jan. 6	Floating and submerged ships and propelling [same.

Name.	Number of Application.	Date of Application.	Subject.

K.

Name.	Number of Application.	Date of Application.	Subject.
Kaberry, L., & Houghton, T.	2206	May 25	Spinning and doubling fibres.
,, L., & Lord, W.	3342	Aug. 25	Cleaning cotton.
Kalbfleisch, F. W., & Sheffield, G. V.	5058	Dec. 30	Uniting boot soles, leather, cloth, &c.
Kalbfleisch, F. W., Sheffield, G. V., & [Fanning, J. (Morgan).	2722	July 1	Boots and shoes; uniting leather, &c.
,, F. W., Fanning, J., & [Sheffield, G. V. (Morgan).	3437	Aug. 31	Sewing-machines for leather, &c.
Kallab, F. V. (Wirth)	3896	Oct. 9	Bleaching animal fibre.
Kamienski, M. (Pitt)	3169	Aug. 10	Treating ores of copper, &c. for metals or salts.
Kamm Co., Hannover Gummi (Wirth)	973	Mar. 6	Bobbins.
Kaselowsky, E. (Alexander)	609	Feb. 15	Dredging-machinery.
Kaufmann, A. F.	210	Jan. 19	Starting cars and vehicles.
Kay, J.	4872	Dec. 16	Drawing-board.
,, T.	1399	Mar. 31	Money-tills.
Kaye, W.	941	Mar. 4	Steam-engines
Kayser, A. & N., & Helwig, J. B., [(Hughes).	3729	Sep. 23	Steam-gauge and safety-valve.
,, N. & A., & Helwig, J. B. [(Hughes).	3729	Sep. 23	Steam-gauge and safety-valve.
Keats, J., & Greenwood, A.	3455	Sep. 1	Boots and shoes and sewing same.
,, J., Neil, J., & Batley, J.	4076	Oct. 21	Boots and shoes and lasting, &c. same.
Keddy, T.	2	Jan. 1	Cutting straw, hay, &c.
Keel, G.	1147	Mar. 16	Roller skates.
,, G., & Pringle, W.	1562	Apr. 13	Roller skates.
Keene, S. D.	3553	Sep. 11	Cotton openers and cleaners.
Keey, W. H.	3434	Aug. 31	Fastenings for boots, shoes, &c.
Kehoe, J., Shauley, T. J., & Driuen, G. C. [(Clark).	2280	May 29	Beer taps.
Keighley, E.	1422	Apr. 3	Singeing fabrics and fibres.
,, E., & Ramsden, J. C.	2281	May 30	Combustion of fuel,
,, J.	3677	Sep. 20	Fog signalling on railways and tramways.
Keim, J.	2956	July 20	Stretching and drying fabrics.
Kelen, L. van der	4563	Nov. 25	Gas-stoves.
Kelly, E. F.	4058	Oct. 20	Portable folding musical instrument.
,, H. W., & Wright, R. L.	5010	Dec. 28	Spinning tobacco.
,, P.	3469	Sep. 2	Combing fibres.
,, S. J. J.	2490	June 15	Producing letters, &c. on glass.
Kelly, W. E. (Lake)	2731	July 3	Harvesting-machines.
Kelman, J. A., & Wilson, J.	3495	Sep. 5	Cleaning tramway rails.
Kelway, C. E.	1455	Apr. 5	Ascertaining rate of vessels, &c.
Kemp, J.	2234	May 27	Screening gravel, coals, &c.
,, R.	3870	Oct. 13	Microscopes.
Kemsley, W.	2587	June 23	Protecting bricks in drying.
Kendal, G.	984	Mar. 7	Bottle-stoppers.
Kendall, H. J. B.	2443	June 13	Attaching braces to trousers.
,, W.	837	Feb. 29	Screwing-machines.
,, W. J., & Whiteley, J.	4498	Nov. 21	Roller skates.
Kennedy, De- L., Delamater, C. H., & [Robinson, G. H. (Lake).	3207	Aug. 14	Punch or projectile.
Kennedy, M., & Eastwood, J.	2233	May 27	Rock-drilling machinery.
,, T.	5013	Dec. 28	Water-meters.
,, T. S.	389	Jan. 31	Drilling-machines.
Kent, A.	2567	June 21	Tooth-brushes.
,, G.	4804	Dec. 12	Cutting or mincing and other machines.
,, G.	4837	Dec. 14	Knife-cleaning machines.
Kenyon, Hartley	1176	Mar. 18	Oxide and chloride of zinc.
,, Henry, & Heron, M.	1628	Apr. 18	Blast furnaces.
,, J. & J. H.	1332	Mar. 29	Extinguishing fire.

184

Appendix VIII

William Wright's Two Patent Applications Nos. 3921 and 4397

A.D. 1875, 11th *November.* N° 3921.

Roller Skates.

(This Invention received Provisional Protection only.)

PROVISIONAL SPECIFICATION left by William Wright at the Office of the Commissioners of Patents, with his Petition, on the 11th November 1875.

I, WILLIAM WRIGHT, of Looe Street, Plymouth, in the County of
5 Devon, Brassfounder, do hereby declare the nature of the said Invention for "IMPROVEMENTS IN ROLLER SKATES AND IN MEANS OF MAKING OR BUILDING UP ROLLERS FOR SKATES," to be as follows :—

The first part of this Invention relates to those skates in which the rollers are set or arranged in the central line of the footboard. According
10 to this first part I arrange four rollers or wheels in brackets fixed to the under side of the footboard; the fore-and-aft rollers are set in the brackets or in separate brackets at a higher level than the two inner rollers, to facilitate by a depression of the toe or the heel portion the production of a curvilinear motion over the surface. The edge of each
15 roller is of rounded or of convex form to enable the skater by a tilting of the footboard to run upon any portion of the rounded part, according to the curve he desires to make. In the motion for producing short curves the skate is tilted at the heel or at the toe, so that the run is then upon either the two front rollers or the two back rollers.

Wright's Improvements in Roller Skates.

According to the second part of my Invention I arrange discs of
leather, wood, or other slightly compressible body between two collars,
the leather or the wood, preferably having a disc of metal or such like
body between, the edge of such disc of metal then serving as the tread
or bearing body to take the principal weight of the skater and as a 5
powerful wear resisting material, the centre of the roller periphery being
more subject to wear than the sides.

The collars are screw threaded on the interior, and take over a piece
of tubing threaded upon the exterior, the tubing being of such a length
that its shoulders act as edge bearers against the inner sides of the 10
bracket to preserve the parallel action upon the axle pin which is
rigidly fixed by nuts on the outer ends, the nuts pressing against the
outer sides of the brackets.

LONDON:
Printed by George Edward Eyre and William Spottiswoode,
Printers to the Queen's most Excellent Majesty. 1876.

A.D. 1875, 18*th* December. N° 4397.

Roller Skates.

LETTERS PATENT to William Wright, of Looe Street, Plymouth, in the County of Devon, Brassfounder and Engineer, for the Invention of " Improvements in Roller Skates."

Sealed the 16th June 1876, and dated the 18th December 1875.

PROVISIONAL SPECIFICATION left by the said William Wright at the Office of the Commissioners of Patents, with his Petition, on the 18th December 1875.

I, William Wright, of Looe Street, Plymouth, in the County of
5 Devon, Brassfounder and Engineer, do hereby declare the nature of the said Invention for " Improvements in Roller Skates," to be as follows :—

This Invention relates to those skates that have two sets of rollers as pairs at the toe and heel of the footboard, the rollers being so arranged
10 that by a canting action of the footboard a cramping action of the rollers will follow to obtain curvilinear or other movements, appliances being fitted to bring the rollers in position again for straight skating.

According to my Invention I form a block or bracket with an inclined flange plate for attaching it to the footboard, toe or heel, as the case may be. The end of a socket on this bracket has an angled or cone-shaped face against or upon which a correspondingly shaped face of a carriage piece bears preferably under the pressure of a spring. This **5** carriage piece has a projecting socket through which the axle pin for carrying the rollers passes, and in which the axle is free to turn in order to have a motion independent of that of the rollers. Through the centre of the first-named socket I fit a tapered pin on which the carriage piece is free to move in a circular direction to the right and to the left, and **10** with a rising motion due to the curve or cone shape of the meeting faces.

A spring is employed between two washers under the carriage piece, on to one of which washers the end of the centre pin is rivetted or otherwise secured to retain it in place.   **15**

Instead of attaching the centre pin to the socket, as before explained it may be part of same.

SPECIFICATION in pursuance of the conditions of the Letters Patent, filed by the said William Wright in the Great Seal Patent Office on the 16th June 1876.   **20**

TO ALL TO WHOM THESE PRESENTS SHALL COME, I, WILLIAM WRIGHT, of Looe Street, Plymouth, in the County of Devon, Brass-founder and Engineer, send greeting.

WHEREAS Her most Excellent Majesty Queen Victoria, by Her Letters Patent, bearing date the Eighteenth day of December, in the year **25** of our Lord One thousand eight hundred and seventy-five, in the thirty-ninth year of Her reign, did, for Herself, Her heirs and successors, give and grant unto me, the said William Wright, Her special license, that I, the said William Wright, my executors, administrators, and assigns, or such others, as I, the said William Wright, my executors, **30** administrators, and assigns, should at any time agree with and no others, from time to time, and at all times thereafter during the term therein expressed, should and lawfully might make, use, exercise, and vend, within the United Kingdom of Great Britain and Ireland,

Wright's Improvements in Roller Skates.

the Channel Islands, and Isle of Man, an Invention for "IMPROVEMENTS
IN ROLLER SKATES," upon the condition (amongst others) that I, the said
William Wright, my executors or administrators, by an instrument in
writing under my, or their, or one of their hands and seals, should
5 particularly describe and ascertain the nature of the said Invention,
and in what manner the same was to be performed, and cause the
same to be filed in the Great Seal Patent Office within six calendar
months next and immediately after the date of the said Letters
Patent.

10 NOW KNOW YE, that I, the said William Wright, do hereby declare
the nature of the said Invention, and in what manner the same is to
be performed, to be particularly described and ascertained in and by
the following statement thereof, that is to say :—

This Invention relates to those skates that have two sets of rollers as
15 pairs, one at the toe and one at the heel of the footboard, the rollers
being so arranged that by a canting action of the footboard on the part
of the skater by a lean over of his foot a cramping action of the rollers
will follow to obtain curvilinear or other movements, appliances being
fitted to bring the rollers in position again for straight skating.

20 According to my Invention which is clearly shown in the annexed
Drawings, I form a block or bracket A with an inclined flange plate B
for attaching it to the footboard C, toe or heel, as the case may be. The
end of a socket D on this bracket has an angled or cone-shaped face E,
against or upon which a correspondingly shaped face of a carriage piece F
25 bears under the pressure of a spring G. This carriage piece F has a
projecting socket H through which the axle pin I for carrying the
rollers J, J, passes, and in which the axle is free to turn in order to
have a motion independent of that of the rollers. Through the centre of
the first-named socket D I fit a tapered pin K on which the carriage
30 piece F is free to move in a circular direction to the right and to the
left, and with a rising motion due to the curve or cone shape of the
meeting faces of the socket and the carriage piece.

The spring G is employed between two washers L, L, under the
carriage piece, on to one of which washers the end of the centre pin is
35 rivetted or held, or otherwise secured to retain it in place.

The tapered pin may be in a piece with the socket, and one washer
may be dispensed with and form part of the block.

Wright's Improvements in Roller Skates.

Having now described the nature of my said Invention and in what manner the same is to be performed, I declare that I claim,—

The inclined faces on the block or bracket piece and on the carriage piece as described when fitted to roller skates, as and for the purposes set forth and substantially as shown.   5

Secondly. I claim the conical or tapered pin on or to a bracket of a roller skate to permit a carriage piece to turn thereon without jam in the rising motion when a skater is performing curvilinear movements as described, and as shown in the annexed Drawings.

In witness whereof, I, the said William Wright, have hereunto 10 set my hand and seal, this Fifteenth day of June, One thousand eight hundred and seventy-six.

WILLIAM WRIGHT.   (L.S.)

LONDON:
Printed by GEORGE EDWARD EYRE and WILLIAM SPOTTISWOODE,
Printers to the Queen's most Excellent Majesty.   1876.

190

APPENDIX IX
NATIONAL SKATING ASSOCIATION RULES

National Skating Association of Great Britain.

Founded in 1879.

RACING BYE-LAWS, AMATEUR AND PROFESSIONAL OPEN EVENTS.

The following provisions shall apply to all Amateur races held under N.S.A. Laws, and to all professional races held by a Committee of the Association.

Track. For four runners the track shall not be less than 15ft. wide on the straight, for six runners 20ft. Curves and turns should, as far as possible, be made symmetrically, that is, that there should be a general curve from the end of one straight to the point where the next straight begins. The track line should be marked in whiting or paint, and be at least one inch wide, and it is from this track that the distance is measured, 18in. from the line going towards the walls of the building. From 3 to 5 tubs to be used at each end to mark the course, failing this, flags at least 5ft. high to be used for marking the course.

Starting. The starter shall place the competitors on their allotted marks, and shall, if necessary, have the assistance of marksmen for this purpose and shall have power to decide all questions respecting starts. If a competitor starts from his mark before the signal has been given, the starter shall put him back 3 yards for distances not exceeding 880 yards, and 5 yards for greater distances. These distances shall be doubled for a second offence. A third offence shall disqualify the competitor. This shall apply to all competitors whether scratch races or handicaps.

Pistol. All races to be started by pistol. The starter shall stand behind the competitors so as to be out of their sight.

Judges. That in all open races 3 Judges shall be appointed the majority of whom shall decide and their decision to be accepted as absolutely final.

Decisions. No decision shall be given by the Judges until they have received the report of the linesmen and lap scorer and scorers.

Other Officials. A starter and lap scorer or scorers shall also be appointed, and in all open handicaps a check starter should be appointed in addition. Sufficient linesmen must be appointed to ensure that competitors keep the course, and they shall report to the Judges any fouls which may occur or any improper action on the part of any competitor.

Racing. The competitor drawing the inside berth has the right of way and can only be passed on the outside, but should he stray from the inside, any competitor is privileged to pass on the inside, providing there is room. The races to be skated left hand inside. No man shall cross to the inner edge of the track unless he is at least 2 yards in advance of his nearest competitor.

Protests. A claim of foul in a race must be made to the Judges immediately after the race, and unless so made shall not be entertained.

That all protests against any competitor, ruling award or other detail must be made strictly in accordance with Rule.

Disqualification. The Judges may disqualify any competitor or competitors who wilfully impede, improperly crosses the course of, or in any way interferes with another competitor, or who, in the opinion of the Judges, conspire with others to cause a race to result otherwise than on its merits. They shall also disqualify any competitor who fails to keep the course. The Judges shall report any such disqualification to the Secretary of the Roller Committee and the Committee shall deal with the offending competitor in such manner as they deem desirable.

That all sentences of disqualification or suspension shall be binding on all clubs affiliated to the Association and all such sentences shall be notified by the Hon. Secretary to the controlling Associations of other Sports with whom the N.S.A. have working agreements.

Entries. Every entry shall be made in the real name of the competitor and no entry shall be made or accepted unless the N.S.A. official entry form be used.

No entry shall be tendered or accepted unless accompanied with the entrance fee.

The management promoting a competition shall have the right to refuse any entry without being bound to assign a reason for such refusal.

Every entry shall be signed by the entrant and he shall be responsible for all statements therein or any omissions therefrom.

Clothing. Every competitor shall be completely clothed and unless properly attired shall be excluded from the competition.

Unattached Competitors. After the first season every competitor in open races under N.S.A. Laws must be a member of an affiliated club or become a member of the N.S.A. direct.

Prizes. A prize awarded to a successful competitor shall be deemed and taken to be so awarded subject to such competitor being eligible to compete and to the statements in his entry form being strictly accurate, and should it be subsequently shown that he was not eligible to compete or that any of the statements in his entry form were inaccurate, any competitor who shall have received a prize to which he was not entitled shall be required to return it forthwith.

Handicapping. That all open handicaps must be made by the N.S.A. Official Handicapper, and no other person other than the Official Handicapper shall at any time alter any handicap mark or allowance allotted by the handicapper unless such alteration is required to correct a clerical or printer's error.

No person shall be entitled to compete in any trial heat other than that in which his name is printed in the programme.

Every event other than as defined in Permit Bye Law No. 5 shall be deemed an open competition, and if a handicap must be handicapped by the Official Handicapper to the Association.

That entries for open handicaps shall close seven days prior to the date of the meeting and shall be forwarded to the Secretary of the promoting body who must despatch the entry forms so that they shall reach the Official Handicapper not later than 6 days before the meeting. The handicapping fee (as per scale) must accompany the entry forms.

N.S.A. PERMIT BYE-LAWS.

As stated in the previous issue of THE WORLD ON WHEELS, the objects of the National Skating Association are the promotion of speed and figure skating, both on ice and roller skates, by means of the establishment of speed skating, championships, and of standards of proficiency and competitions in figure skating, and by such other means as may from time to time be deemed advisable by the Council.

In the same paper was also published the rules recently adopted by the Council of the Association relating to Roller Skating Competitions and defining Amateur Status and also provisions applying to all Amateur races held under N.S.A. Laws and to all professional races held by a Committee of the Association.

In addition to the foregoing the following are the Association's Permit Bye-Laws :—

1. That any club or Promoting body, not affiliated to the National Skating Association, or any person as provided for in Bye-law and wishing to hold a meeting or competition under N.S.A. Laws must make application to the Hon. Secretary of the Roller Committee at least fourteen days previously, for a Permit (on a form to be provided) enclosing a fee of 5s. and stating :

A. Date, place, and time of meeting.

B. Every item on programme.

C. An undertaking to carry out the laws of the N.S.A. in every detail.

2. That all permits shall be signed by the Chairman and Honorary Secretary of the Roller Committee who shall report to the Committee from time to time particulars of permits granted and refused. In the event of a permit being refused the fee of 5s. shall be returned.

3. That no permits be granted to individuals except in cases where a meeting is held in aid of a stated charity which must be approved by the Honorary Secretary, in which case a balance sheet must be produced to him within one month after date of meeting.

4. That no permit be granted for competition at places such as theatres, music halls, circuses, or places of similar entertainments, or to any person who is not an amateur according to the N.S.A. definition.

5. That an affiliated club need not apply for a permit to hold a meeting confined to its own members or a competition which is restricted to the members of not more than two affiliated clubs holding such competition conjointly.

6. That an affiliated club must apply for a permit to hold a meeting in which open events are included in the programme, but that no charge shall be made for same.

The N.S.A. regulations relating to racing, speed and figure skating and the provisions as to the Association Badges will appear in a later issue.

Appendix X

Rules for Instructors

1. Instructors to be on the floor 10 minutes before the Session commences

2. Instructors are not allowed to skate with Patrons without permission from the Manager or Floor Manager

3. All patrons requiring instruction must be referred to the Floor Manager

4. No Instructor must give a lesson unless a ticket has already been purchased and O.K.'d by the Floor Manager

5. No Instructor must leave the floor without permission

6. Instructors must exercise strict care that no objectionable personal features are in evidence, arising out of indulgence in intoxicating drink or smoking

7. Instructors must wear a white tie and white gloves the whole time they are on the Skating Surface

8. When in doubt do not act on your own responsibility. Ask the Manager

9. All lost property found on the rink must be brought to the Manager's office immediately

10. No smoking allowed on the rink

11. Re fast skating, in attempting to stop same do not push or place a hand on anybody as it is dangerous. Simply hold hand up. (Strict Rule)

*(These rules were found in the Cuttings Book of
John Brock, Millbay Rinkeries date c.1910)*

Appendix XI

Census Entry for Thomas Martin 1881

1881 England Census

Name:	**Thomas Martin**
Age:	35
Estimated birth year:	abt 1846
Relation:	Head
Spouse's name:	Harriett
Gender:	Male
Where born:	Plymouth, Devon, England
Civil parish:	Plymouth St Andrew
County/Island:	Devon
Country:	England
Street address:	Somerville House North Rd
Condition as to marriage:	Married
Education:	
Employment status:	to see this information.
Occupation:	Skating Rink Proprieter 3/8
Registration district:	Plymouth
Sub-registration district:	St Andrew
ED, institution, or vessel:	7a
Neighbors:	
Household Members:	Name
	Amy Martin
	Florrie Martin
	Harriett Martin
	Thomas Martin
	Tom Martin
	Willie Martin

Source Citation: Class: *RG11*; Piece: *2196*; Folio: *88*; Page: *27*; Line: ; GSU roll: *1341528*.

Appendix XII

Rinkeries (1909) Ltd Employment Contract

An Agreement made this   day of

One Thousand Nine Hundred and Eight   **Between** THE RINKERIES LIMITED,

The Rinkeries, Aldwych, Strand, London, W.C., hereinafter called "the Company," by their

MANAGING DIRECTOR, of the one part, and

of

in the county of   hereinafter called "the Employé" of

the other part.

Whereby it is agreed as follows :—

1.—That the Company shall employ the said Employé and that the said Employé shall serve the

Company as a

at wages at the rate of   per day, payable on

Saturday in every week.

2.—That the Employé shall not be entitled to any notice of dismissal, but the Company shall be at liberty at any moment, and without assigning any reason whatever, to dismiss the said Employé, and to put an end to the said employment, and thereupon the Company shall only be liable to pay to the said Employé wages calculated up to the time of such dismissal, and at the rate aforesaid.

3.—That the Company shall not be under any liability whatever to pay any damages or compensation to the said Employé for any injury which may be sustained by the said Employé while so employed, either through any act, omission, or neglect of the Company, or through any act, omission, or neglect of any person or persons employed by them.

4.—That in case the said Employé shall at any time be absent from the said employment either through illness or any other cause, such Employé shall not be entitled to any wages for or during the period of such absence.

As Witness the hand of the said parties

Witness to the Signatures

On behalf of Rinkeries Limited,

Managing Director.

THE RINKERIES,
   ALDWYCH, STRAND,
      LONDON, W.C.

APPENDIX XIII
FIELDENS' AUCTION CATALOGUE –
ROLLARENA SKATING EQUIPMENT

SKATE HIRE

1/7.	4 PAIRS DISCO ROLLER SKATES - SUPPOSED SIZE 6
8.	5 PAIRS DISCO ROLLER SKATES - SUPPOSED SIZE 6
9/24.	4 PAIRS DISCO ROLLER SKATES - SUPPOSED SIZE 7
25/26.	5 PAIRS DISCO ROLLER SKATES - SUPPOSED SIZE 8
27/40.	4 PAIRS DISCO ROLLER SKATES - SUPPOSED SIZE 8
41/43.	5 PAIRS DISCO ROLLER SKATES - SUPPOSED D'SIZE 9
44.	5 PAIRS DISCO ROLLER SKATES - SUPPOSED SIZE 10
45/48.	5 PAIRS DISCO ROLLER SKATES - SUPPOSED SIZE 11
49/52.	5 PAIRS CHILDRENS DISCO SKATES - VARIOUS SIZES
53/59.	4 PAIRS DISCO ROLLER SKATES - SUPPOSED SIZE 2
60/54.	4 PAIRS DISCO ROLLER SKATES - SUPPOSED SIZE 3
65/75.	4 PAIR DISCO ROLLER SKATES - SUPPOSED SIZE 4
76/94.	4 PAIRS DISCO ROLLER SKATES - SUPPOSED SIZES 5 & 6
95/96.	5 PAIRS DISCO ROLLER SKATES - SUPPOSED SIZES 5 & 6
97/100.	BIN CONTAINING ODD ROLLER SKATES
101/102.	BOX CONTAINING ODD ROLLER SKATES
103.	CASH REGISTER DRAWER
104.	AUTOMATICKET SYSTEM
105.	3 CHAIRS & 2 STOOLS

WORKSHOP

106.	BOX OF 10 NEW SKATE BASES
107.	PAIR NEW DISCO SKATES - BROWN & FAWN
108.	PAIR NEW BLACK LEATHER SIZE 8 SKATE BOOTS
109.	PAIR NEW BOYS/GIRLS ROLLER DERBY SIZE 2 MODEL US50 ROLLER SKATES
110.	PAIR NEW BOYS/GIRLS ROLLER DERBY SIZE 3 MODEL US50 ROLLER SKATES
111.	PAIR NEW BOYS/GIRLS ROLLER DERBY FIREBALL MODEL 23116 SIZE 12 ROLLER SKATES
112.	PAIR NEW BOYS/GIRLS ROLLER DERBY FIREBALL MODEL 23116 SIZE 10 ROLLER SKATES
113/114.	PAIR NEW CHILDS SIZE 13 RED & BLACK SKATE SHOES
115.	PAIR NEW DEXTER SIZE 5 BLACK LEATHER DISCO SKATES
116.	PAIR NEW RED & BLUE LEATHER SIZE 9½ ROLLER SKATES
117/119.	PAIR NEW ROLLER DERBY FIREBALL CHILDRENS SIZE 10 MODEL 23116 ROLLER SKATES
120.	PAIR NEW ENGLISH PRO 29" BLACK & BROWN LEATHER SKATE BOOTS
121.	PAIR NEW 'WHEELS' SIZE 2 RED & BLUE ROLLER SKATES
122.	PAIR SIZE 3 LADIES SUEDE BOOTS
123.	PAIR NEW SIZE 12 BLACK, RED & BLUE SKATE SHOES
124.	PAIR NEW SIZE 8 BLUE SKATE SHOES
125/126.	PAIR NEW SIZE 12 BLACK, BLUE & TAN SKATE SHOES
127.	PAIR NEW SIZE 12 BLACK, GREEN & WHITE SKATE SHOES
128.	PAIR NEW SIZE 3½ BLACK LEATHER NEW ENGLISH SKATE BOOTS
129.	BOX OF VARIOUS ROLLER SKATES WHEELS
130.	BOX ROLLER SKATE WHEEL AXLES
131/132.	BOX ROLLER SKATE BASES
134.	LARGE QUANTITY USED SKATE WHEELS, PARTS ETC
135.	4 DRAWER BIMAX CABINET AND CONTENTS, SCREWS, NUTS, BOLTS ETC
136.	SMALL COUNTER
137.	SHELF CONTAINING QUANTITY OF USED ROLLER SKATES
138.	TUBES OF PUTTY, PAINT ETC
139.	BEER BARREL, CHAIRS, USED SKATES ETC (ALL UNDER SHELF)

RINK STORE

140.	4 - 1 LITRE BOTTLES ARPAL STERILITE
141.	QUANTITY LIGHT BULBS, POSTER COLOURS ETC
142.	4 PACKETS 12 BOXES MATCHES, OPTIC HOLDERS ETC
143.	BARDIC EMERGENCY LIGHTING EQUIPMENT & EXIT SIGN
144.	1 FREEZER
145.	METAL & WIRE FRAMED DISPLAY SHELVES
146.	QUANTITY OF FAST FOOD PLATES, CONTAINERS
147.	BOXES, SCREWS, BOLTS ETC
148.	BOX COCKTAIL STICKS, ROLLS OF PAPER TOWELLING SERVIETTES ETC
149/150.	1 - 5 LITRE CONTAINER JOHNSON CAREFREE QUARTZ FLOOR POLISH
151.	1 - 5 LITRE CONTAINER JEYES AGRESSOR MULTI-PURPOSE CLEANER
152.	QUANTITY OF PAPER CHIP HOLDERS, CUPS & FAST FOOD CONTAINERS
153.	FULL BOX ½ltr BEVERAGES 3 PINT SIZE COLUMBIAN COFFEE
154.	GOLDEN CRISPY CORN DISPENSER
155.	QUANTITY CHRISTMAS DECORATIONS
156/157.	4 DOZEN CANS PANDA DRINKS ORANGEADE 330ML
158.	P.V.C. SWEET VENDING CONTAINERS ETC
159.	2 SETS ADJUSTABLE SHELVING & 1 FIXED SHELF UNIT

REFERENCES

Chapter One
1. HARWOOD, JA p.39
2. *A comprehensive outline of early skating history is contained in Howard Bass' work, Chapter Two: 'Pioneers and Royalty' pp.24-25. Many Internet websites also cover the history of ice skating and roller skating.*
3. *Oxford English Dictionary Vol.XIII Q-R, p.965*
4. *The Three Towns will be referred to as one conurbation. The districts were amalgamated to form the County Borough of Plymouth in November, 1914, subsequently becoming a City in 1928.*

Chapter Two:
1. The Royal Engineering College at Keyham was opened in July 1880 and finally demolished in the mid-1980s. A full history of the college can be found on Brian Moseley's excellent website www.plymouthdata.info
2. The counties were: Brecknock; Cardigan; Carmarthen; Cornwall; Devon; Glamorgan; Monmouth; Montgomery; Pembroke; Radnor; Somerset; Haverfordwest. Listed in *Kelly's Directory of Devonshire*, 1893.
3. *Navy List 1875*
4. *Dockyard Circular No.22D* of 25th July 1877
5. G. Body *Railways of the Western Region* pp.154-157
6. *Dockyard Instructions, 1875* p.43
7. Advertisement in *Western Daily Mercury* 18 Jan 1870

Chapter Three
1. ROBERTSON, Patrick p.157
2. ibid
3. BASS, Howard: Chapter Two - *'Pioneers and Royalty'* pp.24-25; Various websites on the Internet.
4. Information on Plimpton's skates obtained from Internet websites, and:
   a. J.A. Harwood *Rinks & Rollers* p.41
   b. Gorton Carruth ed. *Encyclopedia of American Facts and Figures*: entry for year 1863
   c. Patrick Robertson *Shell Book of Firsts* p.57

5   Plimpton's original Letters Patent No.2190 together with the drawings were traced from the *Index to names of applicants for patents of inventions: printed and published by order of the Commissioners of Patents under the Act 15 & 16 Victoria (London, 1865)* and inspected at Birmingham City Library.

6   *Western Daily Mercury* 23 February 1875 p.3.

7   *Western Daily Mercury* 16 December 1875 p.2

8   Ibid

9   Patent numbers for these 'pirate' inventors were obtained from *Alphabetical Name Index of Patentees* held in Birmingham City Library

10   *Western Daily Mercury* 4 July 1876

11   *Western Daily Mercury* 7 July 1876 p.1

12   *Western Daily Mercury* 6 January 1876 p.1

13   BASS, Howard p.27; also in Turner & Zaidman

14   Saltash Gazette 10 March 1910

15   *Western Daily Mercury* 23 November 1875

16   *Western Daily Mercury* 7 October 1876

17   *Western Daily Mercury* 23 February 1875 p.2

18   By the early 1930s John Brock, Proprietor of the Millbay Rinkeries, had installed a PARMEKO amplifier with no less than nine loud-speakers. (Details found in a cutting from the national magazine 'World's Fair', no date, c.1930s.)

19   Stentorphone picture, details and Press report, undated (also found in John Brock's *Cuttings Book)*

20   JA Harwood pp.1-3

Chapter Four

1   NSA Rules are pasted into John Brock's *Cuttings Book* – See Appendix IX

2   *Western Daily Mercury* 11 January 1910

3   JA Harwood p.3

4   ibid p.1454. ibid p.11

6   *Western Morning News* 23 November 1875

7   *Western Daily Mercury* 2 December 1875

8   *Rinking booklet* contained in John Brock's *Cuttings Book*

9   *Western Daily Mercury* 2 December 1875

10   JA Harwood p.19

Chapter Five

1   The St James Hall, at 108 Union Street, opened in 1866, mainly as a variety theatre. It could hold 2,500 persons, opened all year round, the Messrs. Livermore being the lessees. (*Eyres Directory*, 1893 p.10.) It sometimes staged circuses, the Western Daily Mercury advertising Powell's Grand Circus on 1st January 1870. In 1921 it became the Savoy Cinema and was one of the first establishments to show talking pictures.

2   *Western Daily Mercury* 17 November 1874

3   *History, Gazeteer & Directory of the County of Devon 1878-9*

4   *Western Daily Mercury* 1 December 1874.

5   GHILLYER, PF & POWER, WJ Entry No.76.

6   WEST DEVON RECORD OFFICE: Ref PH/5. A 19thC survey and plan of Stonehouse Mill and property held on lease by Mr Herbert, drawn by George Perkins, surveyor, shows other properties nearby including the site of the Albert Hall.

7   *Western Daily Mercury* 2 September 1871 p.5

8   A Diorama was a spectacular three-dimensional effect created by a specially painted cloth and carefully focused lighting invented in 1822 by Louis Daguerre in Paris. From the Greek Dia = through; and Horama = view.

9   In bound copies of *St James Hall Playbills*, 1871

10   *Western Daily Mercury* 22 February 1875

11   *Western Daily Mercury* 4 July 1876 (Thomas Martin, age 35, is listed in Plymouth's *1881 UK Census* Ref RG11/2196 as a 'Skating Rink Proprietor'. He lives with wife Harriet(30) and children Amy (6), Florrie (3), Tom (4) and Willie(1) at Somerville House, North Road, in the parish of St. Andrew, Plymouth. He previously lived at 25 Courtney Street.)

12   *Western Daily Mercury* 7 August 1876

13   *Western Daily Mercury* 7 September 1878 p.8

14   There is very little information in Plymouth Local Studies Department or in the West Devon Record Office on the Albert Hall. The building is listed in *Eyre Bros. 1882 Plymouth Directory* at Eldad, Stoke Road, Stonehouse, but other 19th century directories do not list it. Presumably it had a change of use and was destroyed in the Blitz along with many other buildings in the Stoke and Stonehouse areas.

15   *Western Daily Mercury* 16 December 1875

16   *Western Independent* 1954

17   Listed Building No.740-1/54/139. Inspected in February 2005, p.23 of 71, Buildings at Risk Register, Plymouth. (Details are on the Internet)

18   *Western Daily Mercury* 18 April 1876 (Announcement & Report)

19   *Western Daily Mercury* 2 December 1875 p.2

20   *Royal County Directory of Devonshire & Cornwall,* 1878 p.452

21   *Western Daily Mercury* 24 August 1876 p.5

22   *Western Daily Mercury* 1 September 1876 p.2

23   *Western Daily Mercury* 26 December 1876

24   *Western Figaro* 7 November 1877

25   *The Three Towns Almanac* – entry for 19 April 1877

26   *Western Daily Mercury* 19 April 1877 p.1

27   *Western Daily Mercury* 25 April 1877 p.1

28   *Western Daily Mercury* 2 June 1877 p.80

29   *Western Daily Mercury* 18 July 1877 p.1

30   *Western Daily Mercury* 24 April 1880 p.1

31   *Western Daily Mercury* 2 February 1881 p.1

32   *The Three Towns Almanac* – entry for 3 April 1884

33   From www.plymouthdata.info/post offices

34   *Plymouth & Devonport Weekly Journal* 8 December 1859

35   *Western Daily Mercury* 24 October 1874 p.1

36   *Western Daily Mercury* 2 June 1874 p.1

37   *Western Daily Mercury* 8 January 1880

38   *Eyres Bros. Post Office Directory,* 1885 p.128

39   *The Western Figaro* 21 May 1886 p.1

40   *Palace Theatre Ledgers* held by West Devon Record Office, Plymouth

Chapter Six

1   JA Harwood p.1

2   *Oxford English Dictionary* 2nd edn. Vol.13 Q-R; p.265

3   *Doidges Annual,* 1888 p.

Chapter Seven

1   Roller skating history found on numerous websites which outline skating development

2   *Rinking: How-Where-When. A Few Hints on this Popular and Fascinating Pastime.* pp.3-13)

Chapter Eight

1   Ghillyer - entry for 'Palladium, Ebrington Street'.

2   *Western Morning News* 23 November 1909

3   *Rinking: How-Where-When* pp.26-27

4   John Brock *Cuttings Book* p.8 n.d.
5   John Brock *Cuttings Book* p.19 n.d.
6   *Western Morning News* 25 May 1910
7   *Western Morning News* 15 June 1910 p.5
8   *Western Daily Mercury* 20 Sept 1910
9   *Western Independent* 27 May 1952
10 Ainsworth, Robert: 'Showman who gave city a cinema with 3,500 seats' in *Western Morning News* 10 October 1968 p.8
11 Gill, Crispin: 'Seen and Heard' in *Evening Herald* 27 September 1991 p.6
12 Ainsworth op.cit.
13 Ghillyer op.cit.

Chapter Nine
1   *Western Daily Mercury* 8 October 1909
2   *Western Evening Herald* 21 September 1909
3   *Western Independent* 30 October 1909
4   *Western Daily Mercury* 16 November 1909
5   *Western Daily Mercury* 27 November 1909
6   *Western Daily Mercury* 14 December 1909
7   *Sunday Independent* 31 January 1913
8   *Western Daily Mercury* 27 November 1909
9   *Western Daily Mercury* 4 March 1910
10 *Western Independent* 26 December 1910
11 *Western Daily Mercury* 15 February 1910
12 *Western Daily Mercury* 5 November 1913
13 *Western Daily Mercury* 20 June 1910

Chapter Ten
1   *Independent* 26 Dec 1909
2   *Independent* 15 September 1917
3   *Western Daily Mercury* 4 March 1910
4   *Western Morning News* 25 October 1933
5   *Western Morning News* 7 January 1910
6   *Western Daily Mercury* 2 December 1909
7   *Saltash Gazette* 20 October 1910
8   *Western Daily Mercury* 30 November 1909
9   *Western Daily Mercury* 10 May 1913
10 *Western Daily Mercury* 27 May 1910
11 Newspaper cuttings re the swimming baths scheme were found in Brock's *Cuttings Book*, undated 1911
12 *Western Morning News* 7 January 1932
13 *Western Evening Herald* 11 January 1932

14 West Devon Record Office, Ref: 862/213

Chapter Eleven

1   *Independent* 11 September 1911
2   *Saltash Gazette* 6 October 1910
3   *Western Daily Mercury* 8 November 1910
4   *Western Daily Mercury* 30 July 1913
5   *Western Morning News* 4 September 1914
6   *Western Morning News* 17 November 1914
7   *Western Morning News* 5 October 1914
8   *Western Morning News* 14 October 1914
9   *Western Daily Mercury* 11 May 1916

Chapter Twelve

1   *Saltash Gazette* 10 February 1910
2   *Susser Archive* Chapter 4.
3   *Western Evening Herald* 12 September 1988
4   The World's Fair [from *Cuttings Book* n.d.] c.1933
5   [St Leonard's] *Mail & Times* 11 September 1909
6   *Independent* 24 July 1910
7   *Saltash Gazette* 28 July 1910
8   *Western Evening Herald* 6 February 1914
9   Details of the *Thetis* disaster can be found on http/ahoy.tk-jk.net/
    macslog
10 *Western Daily Mercury* 14 March 1910

Chapter Thirteen

1   Twyford p.147
2   ibid
3   Brian Moseley's website www.plymouthdata.info
4   Twyford p.148
5   ibid p.147

Chapter Fourteen

1   *Western Evening Herald* 'I Remember' 6 June 2000
2   *Western Evening Herald* 'I Remember' 18 July 2000
3   Ghillyer & Power p.42
4   *South Devon Times* 25 November 1965
5   *Western Morning News* 9 July 1979
6   *Plymouth Times* 24 December 1980

7 *Western Evening Herald* 3 November 1980 p.6
 Plymouth Star 6 November 1980
 Information on Plymouth Ice Skating Club and other synthetic ice rinks can be found in newspaper cuttings files kept in Plymouth City Library

8 *Western Morning News* 19 June 1981 p.7
9 *Western Morning News* 15 July 1981 p.1
10 *Midweek Independent* 25 February 1982
11 *Western Evening Herald* 12 November 1981 p.8
12 ibid
13 *Midweek Independent* 25 Feb 1982
14 *Western Evening Herald* 19 Nov 1987
15 *Western Evening Herald* 24 Nov 1987
16 *Evening Herald* 4 September 1989

BIBLIOGRAPHY
PRIMARY SOURCES

BROCK, John *Millbay Rinkeries Cuttings Book*, compiled by John Brock, 1909-1939

Census of England and Wales 1901 (County of Devon: Area, Houses and Population) H.M.S.O., 1902

DOCKYARD CIRCULAR 22 D, 25th July 1877

DOCKYARD INSTRUCTIONS – '*Being the revised Dockyard Instructions, 1st July 1875. Published and made available 9th November 1875 from the Admiralty'*. (These Instructions altered as necessary day by day in the form of *Dockyard Circulars*)

DOIDGES WESTERN COUNTIES ILLUSTRATED ANNUAL 1886. Plymouth: Doidge & Co., n.d.

EYRE BROTHERS POST OFFICE DIRECTORY (Plymouth and Devonport District Directory embracing also Stonehouse, Saltash and the District five miles around ...), 3rd edn. London: Eyre Bros., 1885

HARWOOD, J.A. *Rinks and Rollers* London: George Routledge, 1876

HISTORY, GAZETEER AND DIRECTORY OF THE COUNTY OF DEVON including the City of Exeter, 1878-79, 2nd edn. Sheffield: William White, 1879

INDEX to *Names of Applicants for Patents of Inventions*. Printed and published by order of the Commissioners of Patents under the Act 15 & 16 Victoria. London: Eyre & Spottiswood (for 1876).

KELLY, E. R. ed. *THE POST OFFICE DIRECTORY OF DEVONSHIRE AND CORNWALL*. London: Kelly, (for years 1873; 1893).

MATES ILLUSTRATED PLYMOUTH, including Devonport and Stonehouse and Neighbourhood. (Written by Fredk. Hunt, Borough Librarian, Devonport.) Plymouth: Incorporated Mercantile Association, c.1901.

NAVY LIST London: John Murray for H.M.S.O., 1875

ORDNANCE SURVEY MAPS 126 inch to one mile. '*Plymouth and its Environs'*, 1893; 1895

PALACE THEATRE Ledgers held by West Devon Record Office, Plymouth

POST OFFICE DIRECTORY OF PLYMOUTH, STONEHOUSE AND DEVONPORT, STOKE AND MORICETOWN (with a supplement – 'The Devon Advertiser'). Plymouth: John W. Elvins, 1867

RINKING: HOW – WHERE - WHEN? Plymouth: Mitchell & Co., 1910

J.G. Harrod & Co's *ROYAL COUNTY DIRECTORY OF DEVONSHIRE AND CORNWALL*, 2nd edn. Norwich: Royal County Directory Offices, 1878

ST. JAMES HALL PLAYBILLS Bound copies for 1871-72, (including several bills for other venues and towns). Held by Plymouth City Library.

THE THREE TOWNS ALMANAC (Cumulative bound edition 1865-1885 giving 'principle local events for past year ...')

SECONDARY SOURCES

BARNSBY, George *The Standard of Living in England 1700-1900* Wolverhampton: Reed Publ., n.d. (c.1980s)

BASS, Howard *The Skating Years* London: Stanley Paul, 1958

BODY, Geoffrey *Railways of the Western Region* (PSL Field Guide) Cambridge: Patrick Stephens, 1983

ENCYCLOPEDIA OF AMERICAN FACTS AND DATES 8th edn. edited by Gorton Carruth. New York: Harper & Row, 1987

FLEMING, Guy *Plymouth Bygones: sixty years of memories and pictures.* Exeter: Devon Books, 1991

GHILLYER, P.F. and POWER, W.J. *Plymouth Theatres and Cinemas -* limited copies, privately published, 1983. (A bound copy is held in Plymouth City Library's Local Studies Department.)

OXFORD ENGLISH DICTIONARY, Vol XIII (Q-R) 2nd edn. Oxford: Clarendon Press, 1989

SAMBOURNE, R.C. *Plymouth: 100 Years of Street Travel* Falmouth: Glasney Press, c.1980

SHELL BOOK OF FIRSTS new rev. edn. edited by Patrick Robertson. London: Rainbird, 1983

SUSSER, Rabbi Dr. Bernard *The Susser Archive on the History of the Jews in Devon and Cornwall.* (The archives of Rabbi Susser, together with his computer disks, have been placed in the care of Frank Gent of the Exeter Synagogue and can be accessed on the Internet)

TWYFORD, H.P. *It Came To Our Door: the story of Plymouth throughout the Second World War.* Plymouth: Underhill Ltd., 1945

TWYFORD, H.P. *It Came To Our Door*, revised by Chris Robinson. Plymouth: Pen & Ink Publishing, 2005

WOOD, G.H. *Real Wages and the Standard of Comfort Since 1850* in *Journal of the Royal Statistical Society* 73 (1909) and reprinted in E.M. Carus-Wilson ed. *Essays in Economic History*, Vol. III. London: 1962, pp.318-33

NEWSPAPERS AND MAGAZINES

EVENING HERALD
MIDWEEK INDEPENDENT;
PLYMOUTH & DEVONPORT WEEKLY JOURNAL
PLYMOUTH STAR
PLYMOUTH TIMES
SALTASH GAZETTE
SOUTH DEVON TIMES
ST. LEONARD'S MAIL & TIMES
SUNDAY INDEPENDENT
WESTERN DAILY MERCURY
WESTERN EVENING HERALD
WESTERN FIGARO
WESTERN INDEPENDENT
WESTERN MORNING NEWS
WORLD ON WHEELS
THE WORLD'S FAIR

INDEX

214

216